竟已经九十多岁了，
有人能接过这个接力棒。

MY AUTOBIOGRAPHY

我 的 自 传

赵世人 译

———————————— [美]马大任 著

外语教学与研究出版社

FOREIGN LANGUAGE TEACHING AND RESEARCH PRESS

北京 BEIJING

图书在版编目（CIP）数据

我的自传：英、汉／（美）马大任（John T. Ma）著；赵世人译. —— 北京：外语教学与研究出版社，2017.6
书名原文：My Autobiography
ISBN 978-7-5135-8909-3

Ⅰ. ①我… Ⅱ. ①马… ②赵… Ⅲ. ①马大任–自传–英、汉 Ⅳ. ①K837.125.42

中国版本图书馆 CIP 数据核字 (2017) 第 124566 号

出 版 人　蔡剑峰
责任编辑　易　璐
执行编辑　赵妍琦
装帧设计　郭　莹
出版发行　外语教学与研究出版社
社　　址　北京市西三环北路 19 号（100089）
网　　址　http://www.fltrp.com
印　　刷　北京盛通印刷股份有限公司
开　　本　787×1092　1/32
印　　张　7
版　　次　2017 年 6 月第 1 版　2017 年 6 月第 1 次印刷
书　　号　ISBN 978-7-5135-8909-3
定　　价　20.00 元

购书咨询：（010）88819926　电子邮箱：club@fltrp.com
外研书店：https://waiyants.tmall.com
凡印刷、装订质量问题，请联系我社印制部
联系电话：（010）61207896　电子邮箱：zhijian@fltrp.com
凡侵权、盗版书籍线索，请联系我社法律事务部
举报电话：（010）88817519　电子邮箱：banquan@fltrp.com
法律顾问：立方律师事务所　刘旭东律师
　　　　　中咨律师事务所　殷　斌律师
物料号：289090001

Doing calligraphy at Carol's house

作者简介

马大任（1920—　）
美籍华人学者
著名书法家马公愚次子
原籍浙江温州
现居美国旧金山阿拉梅达

曾就读于省立上海中学。
1938 年投笔从戎，服务于陆军第一军。
1939 年入中央大学外文系。
1941 年志愿参加飞虎队，任队长陈纳德的翻译兼译电员。
1944 年中央大学毕业后，考入重庆新闻学院。
1947 年公费留美，次年获威斯康星大学新闻学硕士学位。

自重庆新闻学院毕业后，任国民党中央宣传部国际宣传处驻北平公共关系官员兼英文周刊《重庆新闻》（*The Chungking Reporter*）记者。自威斯康星大学毕业后，入纽约哥伦比亚大学学习国际关系。中美断交后改习图书馆学，曾任纽约布道研究图书馆副馆长、康奈尔大学图书馆中文图书负责人、斯坦福大学胡佛研究所东亚图书馆馆长、荷兰莱顿大学汉学研究院图书馆馆长、纽约公共图书馆中文部负责人。并曾任台湾大学、淡江大学和华东师范大学客座教授，东南大学和长春地质学院兼职教授。

退休后创办"赠书中国计划"（Books-for-China Project），收集北美学人藏书，赠送给中国大学图书馆。2015 年 9 月 3 日纪念中国人民抗日战争暨世界反法西斯战争胜利 70 周年，受邀作为海外嘉宾参加天安门阅兵仪式。

Volunteer Zhu Ping's car

loaded with donated books

作者与一位志愿者站在装载「赠书中国计划」书籍的集装箱前

A volunteer and I standing in front of a container that holds
donated books for the Books-for-China Project (B4C)

Transferring books from the storage container to
the shipping container

将书本从集装箱
内搬至海运箱内

2015年
9月3日，
作者在天
安门广场

At Tian'anmen Square
on 3 September 2015

留影（作者为前排左一）

2015 年 9 月，湖南芷江飞虎队纪念馆前

Seating (Front row, first on the left)
with a group of fellow Flying Tigers
in front of the Flying Tigers Museum,
Zhijiang, Hunan Province, September 2015

Part of the Ma clan in Wenzhou, 2016

2016 年温州马氏家族
部分成员合影

Reading a newspaper on my balcony

作者在自家阳台阅读报纸

My 96th birthday party in San Francisco, February 2016

2016 年 2 月，美国旧金山，作者 96 岁生日聚会

身兼两职，我很奇怪，就问他为什么他能这样做。

罗先生就说：『我这个党史库是真的，「国史馆」是假的。国民政府离开南京的时候李宗仁是「代总统」，他要将「国史馆」搬到他的老家广西。「国史馆」的资料就被装上一部卡车，车向广西开去。半路上卡车被散兵抢去了，车上的资料被当作废纸丢掉了。所以「国史馆」到台湾的时候，一张纸都没有。总不能让人当空头馆长，但是「国史馆」是政府里的一个编制，不能取消。所以我就把那「国史馆」的牌子挂在党史库的门口。其实里面只有党史库的资料，没有「国史馆」的。』

李宗仁不是国民党的总裁，无权保管党史库，所以所有党史库的资料都运到台湾了。

序言

◯ 我不写日记，我家的族谱也在『文革』时流失，所以，当我的三个在美国出生的孩子想要知道他们的家庭背景、我的生活经历和中国当时的环境时，我真的不知道该怎样回答才好。他们坚持要我写一篇自传。面对他们对家、对我、对中国这样的热爱，我实在无法拒绝，所以就动笔了。

这自传是奉『子女之命』而写的，不宜让外人阅读。不过如我一般的老人的自传是现代史的一部分。中国现代兵荒马乱，史料的流失非常严重，这样的自传可以作为史料的补充。

记得 1962 年我第一次回到远东的时候，在台湾看到老校长罗家伦先生。当时罗先生是『国史馆』馆长兼国民党党史库主任委员。国民党退到台湾后，因为规模缩小很多，许多过去的官员都无法找到工作，只好失业。罗先生居然

III

史的教训，还能建立道德的标准。『养天地正气，法古今完人』，从过去圣贤的传记中得到做人的模范。

所以我现在不仅自己写自传，而且鼓励所有的朋友写自传。他们做过很多重要的事情，自传的参考价值要比我的高得多。我这篇小传只是抛砖引玉，希望更多人为自己，为后人，为国家，为历史，都写自传。

现在台湾『国史馆』里的资料都是到台湾后收集起来的。有些部会将它们运到台湾去的资料交给『国史馆』保存，『国史馆』自己也收集不少资料。潘振球当馆长的时候知道我手上有孙中山的女婿戴恩赛写的《孙中山传》的手稿，就要求我同意他把手稿保存在『国史馆』。戴是纽约哥伦比亚大学的法学博士，精通国际法，回国后经常在孙中山先生身旁。他的手稿对孙中山先生和中国近现代史的研究都有很重要的参考价值。

美国图书馆对中国名人档案的收集非常重视。中国近现代史的研究都要利用那些档案。档案的丰富提高了史学研究的水平和学者的学术地位。中国现代史料的流失严重影响了学术研究。

中国人以史为纲。研究历史不仅能够学习历

V

Contents / 目录

Preface

● An autobiography is for someone who is either famous, or rich, or powerful, or important. I am none of these. My autobiography is written at the request of my children who are wonderful and whom I love very much.

▶ I was born in Wenzhou of Zhejiang Province in China on the 22nd day of the second month of the lunar calendar in 1920. China was then poor and weak. Natural and human disasters, foreign invasions and civil wars, poverty and ignorance, and hunger and injustice were part of the people's daily life.

A person growing up in China was lucky if he had not experienced hunger. He was lucky if he had not been robbed. He was very lucky if he had not been cheated. He was very lucky if he could go to school and pass all important examinations. He was very lucky to have good friends. He was very lucky if he had loving parents. He was very lucky if he had good and filial children. I am a very, very lucky person.

Wenzhou is a good place to live. The word "wen" means warm and "zhou" county. So Wenzhou has a warm climate. It is warm in winter and cool in summer. It may have snow once or twice a year. But the snow was not sticky enough for us to build a snowman.

The Ma Clan

I am the second son of my father who was also the second son of my grandfather who again was also a second son. My grandfather had four brothers and one sister. My father also had four brothers and one sister. I have four brothers and one sister, too. Perhaps it is difficult to keep up this kind of family tradition—the second son having five sons and one daughter. Breaking this family tradition, I have only one son and two daughters. But to me, they are perfect.

The Ma family is one of the most prominent families in Wenzhou. We are not the richest family, nor are we the most powerful. But we are known to have a scholastic and artistic tradition which no other family in Wenzhou can match.

My ancestor five generations ago was a *jieyuan* (解元). He began the scholastic tradition of the Ma clan. A *jieyuan* is the No. 1 scholar of the province. In olden days in China, once in three years an imperial examination was held on every administrative level throughout the country. The first 100 persons who passed the examination were given a scholastic degree. Those who passed the district examination received the degree of *xiucai* (秀才). Those who passed the provincial examination earned the degree of *juren* (举人). The first *juren* is called *jieyuan*. In the same year, my ancestor earned his *jieyuan* degree, and his brother also passed the examination and became a *juren*.

Jieyuan Fu

Once a scholar earned a degree, the government gave him a stipend, usually in the form of farmland. He could rent out the land and collect the rent as his income. The higher the degree is, the larger the stipend. The larger the stipend is, the larger the income. With *jieyuan* and *juren* degrees, the two brothers were rich enough to build two huge mansions in the city of Wenzhou. The two mansions stood side by side and together occupied almost half a block in the city.

The mansion of a *jieyuan* was called *Jieyuan Fu*. Above the front gate of *Jieyuan Fu* was a big horizontal board on which were inscribed the two characters "解元" (*jieyuan*). I was born in this *Jieyuan Fu*.

Almost all the members of my grandfather's family and those of his four brothers' families lived in *Jieyuan Fu*, because they were all descendants of the *jieyuan*. Sometimes, as many as 30 people lived in this mansion. There were about 10 children of similar age to mine. I had no difficulty finding playmates among my fellow Ma clansmen. I never played in the streets with strangers. So to my young mind, all men were brothers.

Concept of Life

The innermost part of *Jieyuan Fu* is a courtyard. That was the place where my father Ma Gongyu (马公愚), and his elder brother Mengrong (孟容), practiced their calligraphy and painting. As a child, I loved to watch them practicing. I began to love painting myself and became quite good at it for my age.

China was then very weak. Foreign powers were encroaching upon her. As a very patriotic person, my father did not encourage me to be a painter. He said to me, "Painting and calligraphy cannot save a country. Young men should learn science and technology in order to make the country strong." He also pointed out the importance of scholarship to art by saying to me, "When you grow up, if you are a good scholar and, at the same time, a good painter, people will call you an artist. If you are only good at painting but not in scholarship, people will call you a craftsman." A craftsman is far below an artist in social status. Thus he nipped in the bud my young ambition to be a painter. Since then, the only thing I am allowed to paint is the bathroom. Later, our house needed a new coat of paint. My mother didn't think the artistic level of my painting was high, so she only asked me to paint the bathroom that was seldom seen by the guests.

I studied in the Science Department of the Shanghai Provincial High School, which was by all measures the best high school in China at the time. All its graduates were able to pass the entrance examination of any good university in China. If I graduated, I could go to the best college of science or engineering and be a top scientist someday. However, I was not able to complete my high school education. The Japanese invaded Northern China in 1937 and the full-scale War of Resistance Against Japanese Aggression started. I remembered my father's instruction when I was young that to save the country is more important to one's life than his personal interest. I gave up my high school education in the 3rd year and joined the army as a volunteer. Before I left Shanghai for Shaanxi Province in inland China to join the First Army in the summer of 1938, my father gave me 90 silver dollars. Because of the serious inflation and the reduction of salaries of all civil and military personnel during the early stage of the war, 90 silver dollars were probably more than the annual salary of a full general then.

My Childhood

I had a very fortunate and happy childhood. My parents were not only loving, but also very well-educated.

In order to modernize China, in the early 20th century, the Chinese government established a Foreign School (洋学堂) in each province. It is so called because, unlike the traditional schools that focused on Chinese classics, these schools followed the curriculum of schools in Western countries. Most teachers in such schools were Westerners, usually professors from American and British universities. Students took courses like English, mathematics, physics, and chemistry.

The Foreign School of Zhejiang Province was located at the capital of the province, the city of Hangzhou. Both my father and my first uncle went there to attend that Foreign School— my father majored in English and my uncle in math. This was the most advanced education any student could receive in China at the time.

My mother also received the best education available for girls in those days. In old China, the only way that a girl could receive an education was for her family to hire a private tutor to educate her. Only a rich family could afford that. Some rich families would let some of their poorer relatives' or friends' girls come to be taught by the same tutor. There were no public schools for girls. My mother was very fortunate. The first girls' school in Wenzhou was established just when she was old enough for school. She attended it and graduated as No. 1 in her class. She immediately became well-known as the first graduate of the first girls' school in Wenzhou.

My mother was outstanding for another reason. During her time, all girls of her age had bound feet. They were told that if they did not have bound feet, they would not be able to find a good husband. But my mother, who had received a modern education, refused to have her feet bound. So she became the only girl of her age in Wenzhou who had natural feet. That made her famous as a female revolutionary.

When my mother married my father, although my father was already well-known as a calligrapher, my mother was more famous. As both of them were so well-educated, they took very good care of me and gave me a very happy and healthy childhood. My father subscribed to all the children's magazines available on the market and I had a bookcase filled with many children's books. I also had a lot of sports equipment to play with.

My cousins and young uncles in the same building (*Jieyuan Fu*) often came to borrow books and magazines from me. It seems that I was destined to be a librarian.

Childhood Education

My childhood education was mainly my mother's teaching. Now and then she gave me some classic proverbs and maxims as guideposts for my conduct. For instance, realizing that I hardly did any homework, she emphasized the importance of hard work and industry by citing to me the Chinese proverb, "少壮不努力，老大徒伤悲 (If you do not work hard when you are young, you will be sorry in old age)."

It was quite true that I almost never did homework when I was in elementary school. That was because it was quite unnecessary for me to do homework. I had read many children's books. I read good children's magazines regularly. I had a great deal of basic knowledge—enough to handle all the tests in elementary school. I never crammed for examinations. I never flunked any examination. I even got good grades.

Childhood education includes formal school education, which begins with kindergarten. During my time, Wenzhou had only one kindergarten, which was funded by the Education Department of Zhejiang's provincial government. It was attached to the provincial elementary school and had just a single room that could seat about 20 children. Wenzhou had a population of about two million people then. Every child wanted to attend that kindergarten. In order to get into that kindergarten, a child must pass an entrance examination, which was more or less like an IQ test. Because of the large number of applicants and the limited space of the kindergarten, the acceptance rate was probably the lowest in the world.

When I was five years old, my mother brought me to the kindergarten to take the entrance examination. The yard of the elementary school was crowded with thousands of children. It could take several days to test them all. I was lucky to take the exam the first day I was there. The teacher who tested me sat across a small table and asked me to do all sorts of silly things, such as counting the marbles, drawing a picture, repeating a series of numbers, and recognizing some objects in a picture.

A few days later, the kindergarten published the list of children who had successfully passed the entrance examination and would be admitted to the kindergarten. I was No. 1 on the list.

China has an entrance examination for every level of education—kindergarten, elementary school, junior high school, senior high school, college, and graduate school. I have been very lucky with entrance examinations. I've never failed any of them.

I did not always have good grades at school. I did not always study hard except for in graduate school, when I had to win a scholarship to go to the United States for advanced studies. I always remember the Chinese proverb my mother taught me: "If you do not work hard when you are young, you will be sorry in old age." I am old now, but I do not feel sorry. I am extremely lucky to have three children who work hard themselves and try hard to prevent me from being sorry in my old age.

少年越洋去留学，
没有当官没赚钱。
一生只管图书馆，
退休旧金山湾边，
对街鸟类禁猎区，
无忧小鸟好几千。

后楼 P029

今年马年第一天，

马马虎虎过了年，

昨天没吃年夜饭，

今年年糕也不甜。

做起事来不落后，

赚起钱来不争先，

Selection of Friends

From the balcony of my apartment in Alameda, California, I can see many birds in the bird sanctuary across the street. There are black birds and white birds, but they never mix. It is a concrete example of the proverb, "Birds of a feather flock together." There is a Chinese proverb "物以类聚," which means exactly the same thing. The Chinese use that proverb to teach children how to select friends. Selection of friends is one of the most important things in education because children learn many things from their friends. And many children are influenced by friends more than by anyone else. My experience in junior high school is a good example of such influence.

When I began my first semester in junior high school in 1932, I followed the same habit as I had in elementary school. I did not do homework. I spent a lot of time playing sports and games. One of my best friends was a boy from an underdeveloped area in my province. He had never seen a big and modern city like Wenzhou. So he was quite excited about many things in Wenzhou, and liked to see or experience them. He often asked me to go and play with him. So I missed many classes and, as a result, flunked two of the most important courses—English and math. I was held back that semester.

When my mother found out the reason for my failure, she sought out a classmate of mine, Zeng Shouzhong (曾守中), who was a good student. His family was fairly well-to-do when he was younger. Then his father suddenly passed away. He realized that someday he would have to support his whole family. That made him very mature. He studied very hard. He never wasted any time or money. After the passing of his father, he moved to live in the house of a distant relative of my mother. One day my mother took me to see this relative and meet Shouzhong. She asked him to be my friend and he did. From then on, I spent most of my time with him. We studied together and played together. My grades went up and I passed all the examinations. By the time I reached the third year, which was the last year in junior high, I became the only student in the class who was an honor student for all three categories—academics, sports, and social conduct.

After graduation, I went with three classmates to Shanghai and tried to take the entrance examination of Shanghai High School. That was definitely the most difficult high school in China to enter. I was the only one from Wenzhou who was admitted to that school that year. Thanks to Shouzhong, I had turned from a black bird into a white bird.

The War

The Chinese People's War of Resistance Against Japanese Aggression, known in vernacular Chinese as *Kang Ri Zhanzheng* (抗日战争) or *Kang Zhan* (抗战), is by all measures the most significant event in the history of modern China. It lasted 14 years—8 years longer than World War II, and incurred many more casualties. It affected the life of almost everyone in China, me included.

The full-scale war started in 1937, when I was a student in the Science Department of Shanghai High School. It dashed my aspiration to be a scientist.

The warlords of Japan had the ambition to conquer the whole world. In order to achieve this ambition, they had to conquer China first. In 1931, they created the Mukden Incident to occupy Manchuria. In 1937, the Japanese troops tried to enter the city of Peking by crossing the Marco Polo Bridge. As the Chinese troops resisted, a full-scale war broke out.

The Chinese government knew that sooner or later Japan would invade China. In preparation for resistance against the impending Japanese invasion, the Chinese government ordered all students who had completed the first year of senior high school to receive a three-month military training. When the Marco Polo Bridge Incident happened, I was in the military training camp at Zhenjiang, capital of Jiangsu Province. The officers who were training us were from the 88th Division, a crack division of the Chinese Army.

Every morning the Brigade Commander, who was in charge of the daily operation of the training camp, would preside over the morning exercises and give us a short speech. One day he did not show up. Later I learned that he had gone to Shanghai to inspect the military situation there. Japan had started to invade Shanghai.

When I went to the military training camp in 1937, I went directly from my school in Shanghai to Zhenjiang. I had left all of my luggage at school. When I returned to Shanghai a few months later, I could not go to my school to retrieve my luggage because the campus was located in the Chinese territory, while my home was in the French Settlement. Because of the war, all roads from the foreign settlements to the Chinese territory were blocked. I lost all of my luggage as a result, including my tennis racquet, my most precious possession. Later the Japanese converted my school into barracks. I do not know which lucky Japanese soldier got my tennis racquet.

Joining the Army

The Japanese troops occupied Shanghai High School. I had no school to attend, so I returned to Wenzhou and continued my education at Wenzhou High School. But not long afterwards, the Shanghai Academy of Fine Arts, located in the French Settlement, let Shanghai High School use their classrooms in the morning. I returned to Shanghai and resumed my education at Shanghai High School.

When the Chinese troops withdrew from Shanghai, they purposely left behind one battalion in a big building across the Suzhou River north of the International Settlement in order to delay the Japanese troops' march on Nanjing, the national capital then. The troops of this battalion came to be known as "800 heroes." Actually, a normal battalion has only 400 soldiers, not 800. Making pretenses of power, the defending battalion claimed to be a regiment and the Chinese government promoted the chief of the battalion to the position of Regimental Commander. The Commander's name was Xie Jinyuan (谢晋元). He was buried in Shanghai. My father wrote the inscription on his tombstone.

Commander Xie was my regimental chief when I received military training in Zhenjiang before the war. When he and his troops were defending the building against the Japanese attack, some bullets landed in the International Settlement. In order to insure the safety of the people in the settlement, the authorities of the International Settlement negotiated with the Japanese for the disarming and transfer of the "800 heroes" to the International Settlement. Commander Xie and his troops were allowed to relocate to an old barrack protected by foreign soldiers. My classmates and I, who were all his trainees, would go to see him every weekend and bring him and his soldiers food and things they needed.

We also engaged in some other kinds of patriotic and anti-Japanese activities. This naturally irritated the Japanese, but they could not send troops into the foreign settlements to attack us. So they began to kidnap students. One day, the newspapers reported that the Japanese had kidnapped a Chinese student and took him to the Japanese Settlement. This worried my father. He told me that if I wanted to continue my education in Shanghai, I'd better live like an obedient citizen (*dang shunmin*, 当顺民), and that if I wanted to leave Shanghai, I would become a refugee (*dang nanmin*, 当难民). I told my father that I wanted to be neither an obedient citizen nor a refugee. I said I wanted to become a soldier (*dang bing*, 当兵).

To the First Army (I)

One day in 1938, a young man by the name of Huang Songhe (黄诵和) came to see my family. He claimed to have come from inland China and brought with him news about my elder brother David (马大恢). David was a student at Nankai University in Tianjin when the war broke out. Together with students of Peking University and Tsinghua University, Nankai students were supposed to move to Kunming, in Yunnan Province, to form the Southwestern Union University. On their way to Kunming, many of them stopped by the city of Changsha and formed the Changsha Temporary University (长沙临时大学). To help the war efforts, some young people had volunteered to join the army or organized a war area service corps. Some students of the Changsha Temporary University had also organized a war area service corps and were ready to go to the front. David was one of them.

At that time, the First Army, under the command of General Hu Zongnan (胡宗南), had withdrawn from Shanghai to Wuhan. When he heard that students of Changsha Temporary

University had a war area service corps, he wanted that corps to become part of the First Army. So he sent a young Hunanese officer to Changsha to meet the leader of that corps and to persuade the corps members to go to Wuhan to see General Hu. His mission was successfully accomplished. And the corps went to Wuhan to meet General Hu.

In Wuhan, General Hu told them that the First Army would move to Shaanxi Province with headquarters in Xi'an. The corps would be named the First Army War Area Service Corps (第一军随军服务团, mentioned as *Fuwutuan* in the following chapters). The main responsibilities of the corps were (1) helping mobilize the people to join the War of Resistance Against Japanese Aggression, and (2) helping educate the local teachers and officials. The corps was divided into small groups. Each group took care of one village. The headquarters of the corps was located in the city of Fengxiang. The corps leader reported directly to General Hu. Local officials and military officers were all very cooperative. My brother David was healthy and doing fine, Huang told us. All members of my family were very happy to hear that.

Huang was scheduled to return to the First Army in a few days. This was the best opportunity for me to join the army. So I told my father that I intended to go with Huang to see David and join the First Army. My father readily accepted my request and I got ready for the long journey.

三个儿女都孝顺，

好友时常来聊天。

乐天知命心常乐，

过了一年算一年，

人生到此无所求，

不是神仙胜神仙。

老年创业收西书，

送给大陆青少年，

让他知道大世界，

也让外语好一点。

少时不学棋书画，

老来补写诗百篇，

Leaving Home

Before I left with Huang for inland China, my experience was limited to just a small part of the south-eastern coastal area. I knew almost nothing about the outside world. But since Huang was a college graduate, my parents trusted him and believed that he would take good care of me.

In order to go to inland China, I first had to take a boat to Hong Kong. Since there were so many people in Shanghai who wanted to leave, it was not easy to get a ticket. Every boat was overbooked. Almost all the passengers were going to inland China. So the boats were called "refugee boats."

Huang had two female friends who wanted to travel with him to inland China. One, like me, wanted to join the First Army and the other just to see her friends. Luckily all four of us got tickets and we went aboard together.

The boat was so crowded that we could not find a room or even a bed. It would take two days for the boat to reach Hong Kong.

We had to find a space to lie down. Finally we found on the deck a space that was large enough to put down two blankets. So the girls took one blanket, and Huang and I the other.

As the boat sailed down the Huangpu River towards the ocean, it passed by a Japanese gunboat that was anchored off the river near the Japanese Settlement of Shanghai. The Japanese ordered all boats to be covered up so that the passengers would not be able to see the guns on the gunboat. It was quite unnecessary because that gunboat had been there since the summer of 1937. All people in Shanghai had seen it.

After two days and two nights, we arrived at Hong Kong. As we were leaning against the railing of the boat and admiring the beautiful harbor of Hong Kong, I asked one of the girls which school she attended in Shanghai. She said Wuben Girls' School (务本女中). Then I asked her how she got to know Huang. She said that Huang was her classmate. I asked her how come that Huang could be in a girls' school. She asked me, "Don't you know Huang is a girl?" I said no. So they all laughed. I had been sleeping with a girl under the same blanket for two nights and did not know she was a girl. Then they asked me to look at Huang's throat and said, "Did you see a lump like a bone sticking out?" I said no. Then they said, "A girl has a flat throat and a boy has a lump." This was the first lesson I learned after I left home. That is, how to distinguish a man from a woman.

Travel in Wartime China

After disembarking at Hong Kong, we immediately went aboard a boat to go to Canton. From the harbor of Canton we took a taxi to the railroad station to buy train tickets for inland China. We were surprised to find that the door of the railroad station was open but not a single soul was in sight. We could not buy any ticket, but there was a train in the station. So we climbed into the train and found seats to sit down and rested.

After about half an hour, a lot of people came into the station. They were surprised to find the four of us seated in the train. We had entered the station when there was an air raid. The Japanese airplanes were bombing Canton. Everybody was supposed to go to the air raid shelter. But we did not know. So we just sat in the train. Luckily the Japanese did not bomb the railroad station. Otherwise, we would have been four casualties of the war.

In order to avoid Japanese bombing, the train ran only at night, not during the daytime. There was no dining car in the train. Nor was there any food for sale. When the train arrived at a station of a city or village, there would be vendors gathering outside the windows of the train, trying to sell us a variety of food. Those vendors were poor peasants and their wives and children. They wore dirty clothing and had dirty hands. As a boy from Shanghai who had never eaten any food except what was cooked by his mother, I could not take anything sold by those people.

It would take two days and two nights for the train to reach the city of Changsha, which was our first stop. I had to eat something. Then I discovered that some peasants were selling lychee and longan. Those shelled fruits were clean. So I bought several boxes of them and ate them all throughout the trip from Canton to Changsha. For two days and two nights I had no starch but plenty of vitamin C in my body.

In Changsha

We stopped by Changsha on our way to the First Army in Shaanxi Province because two members of *Fuwutuan* were taking home leave at Changsha. They wanted us to stay in their house to rest for a few days before continuing our long journey to Shaanxi.

Their house was in the center of Changsha. On the same day we arrived at Changsha, the Japanese airplanes bombed the Eastern Railroad Station of Changsha. There was no air defense in Changsha. Our friends were afraid that we might get killed by the Japanese bombers. So they took us to their country house in their native village east of Changsha. The village had the same name as their family name—Cao. It was called Caojiaping (曹家坪), which means "a level ground of the Cao Family."

They were obviously the largest landowner of the village. Their house was huge. Soon after we arrived, they gave us a banquet with many dishes. The food was colorful and smelled good. I was very hungry and took a big piece of fish as soon as we sat down to eat. The fish tasted funny, not like the taste of any fish I'd had before. I dared not swallow it. Then I took a piece of pork. Strangely enough, it tasted the same as the fish. It was as pungent as red pepper. It was so hot that it burned my tongue, made my nose run, and my eyes shed tears. I could not eat anything but rice.

My hosts realized that I did not eat spicy food. But there was nothing they could do. All the dishes they had prepared for us were hot. The village had no store that sold fresh foods. They could buy fresh foods only during the market days which came every three days in ten days. None of the days during which we were there was a market day. So for three days I ate nothing but plain rice.

Before I left home, I did not know what spicy food was. Chinese food has five tastes (flavors)—sweet, sour, bitter, pungent, and salty. Wenzhou people do not eat pungent food. As a true Wenzhounese, I do not have a full palate.

九六自嘲

今年已经九十六，可以算是蛮长寿。

糊里糊涂过一生，思想文化都落后。

读书总是不甚解，政治不懂左和右。

不出风头不吹牛，不会拍马不争斗。

后接P048

To the First Army (II)

After a few days of rest, I proceeded to go to the First Army in Shaanxi Province. The Commander of the First Army, General Hu Zongnan, had designated the District of Fengxiang as the headquarters of *Fuwutuan*. Next to Xi'an, capital of the province, Fengxiang was the largest county in Shaanxi. But we could not reach Fengxiang by train because it was not on the railroad. We had to get off the train at the nearest station. But the station was so small that we had no place to sit down to rest and eat. So, as soon as we got off the train, we decided to complete the rest of the journey on foot.

As luck would have it, it was raining cats and dogs when we got off the train. The loess of Shaanxi became very soft in the rain. The road became a shallow rivulet. As I walked on the road, with every step I was knee-deep in the mud. It was impossible to walk fast. I put my luggage on a cart pulled by a cow, which was the only transportation means available. The cow walked even slower than I did. She was so weak that I had to stop to push the cart now and then. It took me almost a whole day to cover the 10-*li* (5-kilometer) distance from the railroad station to the city of Fengxiang.

Having walked so long under the pouring rain, I was completely exhausted when I reached the headquarters of *Fuwutuan*. Among the members of *Fuwutuan* there were two doctors. But they had no medicine. Out of fear that I would catch a bad cold, they boiled some water with ginger and brown sugar in it. They gave me that ginger tea to drink. It was good and I fell asleep soon after I drank it. By the time I woke up, I was as good as new.

I learned a lesson in Chinese medicine: ginger tea with brown sugar can prevent one from catching a cold.

The Second Opium War

General Hu Zongnan assigned the District of Fengxiang as the field of operation of *Fuwutuan*. We members of *Fuwutuan* were stationed in various parts of the district with our headquarters in the center of this walled city.

The main responsibility of *Fuwutuan* was to mobilize the people to fight the War of Resistance Against Japanese Aggression. But the educational level of the people was so low that it would take a long time to make them understand what *Kang Zhan* meant. For instance, during the war, the derogatory term we used for the Japanese was *Dongyang Guizi* (东洋鬼子, Ghosts of the Eastern Ocean). One of the peasants asked us, "How could we human beings fight against ghosts?" Another peasant said, "War is Empress Dowager's business. Why should we get involved?" This shows how much educational work we had to do in order to make the people understand the war.

Fuwutuan had only about 35 members. It was impossible for us to educate the people of the whole district. So we started by educating the educators, i.e., teachers of the elementary schools of the district. We set up several training classes for those teachers. After we finished the training of the teachers, we educated *Bao* and *Jia* Chiefs (保长、甲长) who were the lowest-ranked administrators of the district. We hoped that through them the people would be better educated.

But there was one thing we had overlooked. Many people in inland China were opium smokers. To prevent the spread of opium smoking, the Chinese government had made stringent laws. All growing, trading, and smoking of opium were prohibited. Growers and traders of opium would receive capital punishment. And opium smokers would be jailed. Everybody was aware of these laws.

Because oil was expensive, Fengxiang was completely dark at night, with no street lights, nor any door lights. But there was light in front of one store. It was the opium den.

When we discovered this outrageous phenomenon, we immediately sent a report to General Hu and asked him to execute the owner of that opium den and the magistrate of the district. General Hu had the authority to do that. But during the war, to execute the magistrate of the largest county in the province was a very serious business. He had to find a way to save the magistrate's life and, at the same time, provide a satisfactory reply to our report.

Under General Hu there were a number of political officers who could give him political advice. He could send one of them to talk with us. But General Hu knew that his political advisers were no match for us *Fuwutuan* members, as some of us were the best students from the best universities in China. He needed a much better adviser. Finally he found Professor Miao Fenglin

(繆凤林) who was a well-known historian and a professor of the National Central University. He asked Professor Miao to go to Fengxiang to talk with us. Professor Miao agreed.

Professor Miao came to Fengxiang and gave us a lecture. Since we were all volunteers who gave up our studies to join the army, he began by praising us for our self-sacrifice and patriotic spirit. Then he gave us a brief summary of the history of Sino-Japanese relations and the strategy of the War of Resistance Against Japanese Aggression. Finally he told us that war was very expensive business and that the Chinese government was in desperate need of money to support the war efforts. Without foreign trade and with very little industry, the main revenue of the provincial government during the war came from local taxes. As the largest county of the province of Shaanxi, Fengxiang was a big tax-payer. And 80 percent of the Fengxiang tax revenues came from that little opium den. If the owner of that opium den were to be executed and the den closed down, Fengxiang's contribution to the war would be drastically reduced. The execution would have a serious impact on the inland China opium trade and the income of the government. The Chinese government might not be able to carry on the war. Then Professor Miao told us that the only choices were to close the opium den and execute the magistrate, or to continue to support the war. He asked us to make our choice. We all kept silent.

Disbandment of the Service Corps

Members of *Fuwutuan* were quite successful in establishing relations with the local people. There were about 35 members who were distributed to several townships and villages. In addition to our normal educational work, we set up a few health stations to provide rudimentary medical services to the local people. We received some medicines from the First Army. We gave poor patients medicines free of charge. Among the members were two medical doctors and several nurses. We included health information in our educational work. People were very grateful to us for providing them with free medical service. The local people trusted us. They knew that we had direct contact with General Hu, the most powerful government authority in the area. So they often asked us to solve their problems with the government.

People's trust in us naturally raised the jealousy of local officials and political officers of the First Army. By presenting people's complaints directly to General Hu, we had invaded the jurisdiction of those officials and officers. One day we received a call from General Hu, asking all of us to go to his headquarters in Xi'an.

General Hu alone met us in a meeting room. Beside him was a high pile of documents. He pointed at that pile of documents and said, "Those are all reports from my intelligence officers. They say that you are all Communists."

This was a serious accusation. Although Communists and Kuomintang were jointly fighting against the Japanese at that time, Communists were not allowed to be in the Kuomintang army nor government. General Hu had the special responsibility to prevent young people from going to Yan'an (延安), the Communist headquarters, to join the Communist army. He certainly could not have Communists in his own army.

Then he admitted that we were patriotic youth who gave up our good education to serve as volunteers in the army. He could not punish us. So he decided to give us the following three choices:

First, if we wanted to return to school to continue our education, he would pay for our travelling expenses and tuition. If we wanted to go home, he would also defray our travelling expenses.

Secondly, if some of us were Communists and wanted to go to Yan'an to join the Communist army, he would ask his troops who were blockading the road to Yan'an to let them pass.

Thirdly, if we wanted to stay in the army, he would set up a special training class for us. Once we graduated from that class, we would be General Hu's students. Nobody could call his students Communists.

As soon as we made our choices, the meeting closed. And *Fuwutuan*, which had lasted for nine months, was disbanded. Thus my military service in the First Army came to an end.

衣食都是很简朴，不吃大鱼和肥肉。

出门没有小汽车，住家也是很简陋。

无事在家写写字，有书赶快就去收。

好书就送到大陆，帮助学生和教授。

大陆大学很缺书，好书尤其很不够。

如果教育弄不好，国家就永远落后。

社会不会很和谐，百姓也不会得救。

不管你有多少钱，不管你有多长寿，

文化水平不提高，国际形象还是臭。

2015年7月9日 作者写于美国加州阿拉梅达

The Special Training Class

During the full-scale War of Resistance Against Japanese Aggression (1937-1945), in order to train political officers, the Chinese government established four Wartime Political Officers Training Corps. The Fourth Corps was under the command of General Hu Zongnan. It was located in Xi'an, capital of Shaanxi Province. To give us members of *Fuwutuan* special training, General Hu set up a special class within the Fourth Corps of Wartime Political Officers. It was called the Third Class of Trainees of the Fourth Corps. Trainees were considered a cut above the regular students. The Trainee Class had its own campus and dormitory. We did not live on the campus of the Fourth Corps.

Realizing that some of the *Fuwutuan* members had been influenced by Communism or leftist thinking during their school days, General Hu assigned two prominent ex-Communists as our instructors. They taught us the history of communism and that of the Communist Party of China (CPC), and told us about their personal experiences in the CPC and some stories about CPC leaders. Their lectures were quite interesting.

After three months of training, we graduated and were assigned to do various kinds of political work in the armed forces. I was granted the rank of Second Lieutenant and worked in the Second Section of the Political Department of Generalissimo's Xi'an Headquarters, which was the highest authority in Northern China during the war. General Hu was the Head of this Political Department. Mr. Yang Erying (杨尔瑛) was the Head of the Second Section. Yang was a Russia expert and spoke fluent Russian. He told us about his experience as an interpreter for Russian air force pilots who helped China during the early stage of the War of Resistance Against Japanese Aggression. He did not know much about political work. But he was a good businessman. When the Kuomintang troops withdrew to Taiwan in 1949, he purchased a huge apartment building in Taipei and rented out the apartments to those who fled the mainland of China. The building was always fully occupied. And he collected a lot of rent and became quite rich. Whenever I visited Taiwan, he would give me a big banquet.

One of my instructors at the Training Class of Political Officers was the advisor to the Second Section. Actually he, not Mr. Yang, was the one who directed the political work of the Section. His first assignment to us was to survey social organizations in the city of Xi'an. We discovered that Xi'an had a large number of social organizations unknown to many people. Many of them were established during the Northern Expedition when Kuomintang and Communists joined forces to fight against the warlords in Northern China. When the two parties split in 1927, pro-Communist organizations went underground or became dormant. Some leaders of those organizations were still alive when we were doing the survey. Some were still community leaders who could be very useful in mobilizing the people for the war.

War was not all war. The northern front was quiet for quite

a long while. In September 1939, I decided to resume my education. With General Hu's permission, I resigned from the Political Department and went to Chongqing to participate in the unified entrance examination for college. General Hu gave me the money for my travel expenses. I took a bus from Baoji at the end of the railway line to the wartime capital Chongqing.

The bus ride was long and passed through some mountainous areas. When the bus climbed over a mountain top, I smelt an odor. Then tears rolled from my eyes and my nose began to run. I recalled that a person was frying hot pepper when our bus passed by his house. The pepper was so hot that the smell could make you shed tears. I also recalled that there was a row of chili peppers hanging in front of his house. It seemed that hot pepper was the main food ingredient of the poor people in the mountains.

Then I saw two holes in a wall along the road. The distance between the two holes was exactly the distance between the front and back carriers of a sedan. The sedan was the most important mode of transportation in rural areas. It required two persons to carry a sedan on their shoulders. They often shouldered a sedan for a long distance and many carriers used opium to maintain their stamina. It was quite troublesome to put down the sedan and go into an opium shop. So they stopped alongside the wall, turned their heads and positioned their mouths just in front of the two holes. An opium pipe would come out of each hole and allow them to inhale. They just stood there for a bit and then continued to carry the sedan, after getting a boost from the opium.

Clothing, food, housing, and transportation are the four essential necessities of people's livelihood. I had the opportunity to observe first-hand how the poor inland people coped with the necessities of life during the war. It made me wonder which was more important—to win the war or to raise the living standard of the people.

Choosing a Major

A fter a two-day bus ride from Baoji, with a short stop-over in Chengdu, I arrived at the wartime capital Chongqing to participate in the entrance examination for college. At that time China had a unified examination system for all applicants of public universities. Private universities could have their own entrance examinations. The National Central University (NCU) was the largest university in China then. A well-known private university, Fudan University, was also in Chongqing. I applied to both of them. In the unified examination system, applicants were divided into three groups: Group I—science and engineering; Group II—medicine and agriculture; and Group III—humanities and social sciences. Remembering my father's instruction when I was young, I fully intended to study science or engineering to help make China strong and rich. And I was a science student in high school. But my application to Group I was rejected, because the Group I examination included calculus as a required subject, which I never took. It was a course taught in the third year of high school. I never attended the third year of high school because I had joined the army. I would have gotten a "0" for calculus if I had taken the Group I examination.

So I decided to apply for Group Ⅲ with the History Department of the National Central University as my first choice. Before I submitted my application, I asked for advice from a junior student of that department, Mr. Wang Lin. He advised strongly against my selection of the History Department. His reason was that the purpose of studying history was to know the whole world, not China alone. Therefore I must study a foreign language first. Following his advice, I chose the Department of Foreign Languages of NCU as my major. At Fudan University I applied for the Department of Geography and History. I passed the entrance examinations in both Fudan and NCU. Since the NCU was free and Fudan charged tuition, I, as a poor refugee student, entered NCU.

Actually, I entered NCU long before I passed the entrance examination. When I first arrived in Chongqing, I had no place to stay. So I went to see Ms. Ma Xiuquan, the younger sister of Professor Ma Xingye, who was one of my father's students in high school. Xiuquan was then a senior student at NCU and lived in the NCU dormitory. When I told her that I needed a place to stay, she said that she would find a bed for me in the dormitory. There were some vacant beds in the dormitory of senior students because they were either married or had found a job, and had moved out. So I lived like a senior student even before I was a freshman at NCU.

A Hermit Freshman

I started my freshman year as a hermit. The National Central University put its freshmen in a branch campus located in a village called Baixi. Baixi was almost completely isolated from the outside world. It had a population of almost zero. I found only one small shop on the road from the river bank to the campus. The shop owner and his family took care of the shop. Besides these folks, I saw now and then farmers' wives coming to pick up laundry from my schoolmates. I did not know if they lived in the village. Those were the only people I saw in Baixi. The rest were all people of the National Central University—the freshmen, faculty, and staff.

Baixi itself had no roads. To get into or out of Baixi, we had to walk on a small country path and climb over a mountain. The teachers who had to teach on both the main campus and the branch would take a sedan instead of walking. The sedan was carried by two footmen. We students could not afford such luxury.

There was another way to get out of Baixi. That was by boat. Baixi was situated along the Jialing River that ran from the mountains in northern Sichuan and joined the Yangtze River at Chongqing. Now and then a steamboat would sail down the river and pick up passengers from the cities along the river. But Baixi had no pier for the steamboat. In order to go aboard the steamboat, we had to hire a sampan to row to the side of the steamboat and climb aboard. It was not an easy process because the steamboat did not slow down for us.

We could not take boat rides all the time because the Jialing River was usually too shallow for the steamboat. Only during the summer or in a rainy season could the steamboat sail. And the boat ride could be quite dangerous because the boat was capsized quite often.

The Jialing River had many sharp twists and turns. In order to avoid the claustrophobia of being enclosed in a cabin, most passengers liked to stand on the top deck of the boat, which resulted in the boat being top-heavy all the time. This in turn often led to capsizing when the boat made a sharp turn at a curve.

There were usually some sampans along the river. And some could be close to the capsized boat. The sampans could easily pick up a number of passengers in the water, but almost nobody was saved, because the Sichuan boatmen were very superstitious. They believed that, if Yama (the King of Hell) had selected a person to be drowned, the one who tried to save the drowning person was acting against the will of Yama. For that reason, Yama would select him as a replacement for the person saved and he would soon die. So nobody dared to save a person from drowning. That was the risk of taking a boat ride.

The only way to save myself from being drowned when the boat capsized was to know how to swim. So I had to learn how to swim before I took any boat ride. Baixi did not have a swimming pool. And there was no one who could teach me how to swim. So I went to the beach and found a place where the water was shallow. I tried to learn swimming all by myself and eventually I learned how. I did not swim fast, but I learned to swim a long distance. Once I had learned to swim a distance of 400 yards (nearly 366 meters), which was the width of the Jialing River, I felt safe enough to take a boat ride because I could swim to the shore, no matter where the boat capsized.

Sometimes I took a ride in a big wooden boat that carried tangerines downstream to the city of Chongqing. It was a pleasure to ride on one of those boats because the owner would let me eat as many tangerines as I wanted, free of charge. The only condition was that I must leave the tangerine skin on the deck, and not throw it into the river. The reason for that is that the tangerine skin could be used as herbal medicine. When the boat arrived at Chongqing, the owner had to hire people to peel the tangerines for him to sell the skin. So, as we were eating tangerines free of charge, we were also peeling the tangerines free of charge. That was a fair exchange.

Life at Baixi was hard. The government did not give us enough rice to eat. We had to fight for rice at almost every meal. If we were not successful in getting a bowl of rice, we grew hungry. Fortunately, Sichuan Province produced lots of tangerines and peanuts. They were inexpensive and nutritious. They helped to keep us half-starving freshmen alive and healthy.

My Sophomore Year

After completing my freshman year, I left Baixi for the main campus at Shapingba (沙坪坝) in Chongqing as a sophomore. And I suffered no more. We had enough rice to eat. We had a place to take a shower. And I could go to many places by bus. There was even an airline with flights to several major cities. Most important of all, we learned something about the war. That is, air raids.

Baixi had no air raids. Chongqing had two kinds of air raid— the terrifying raid and the tiring one. During the terrifying raid, a number of bombers bombed the same place. All people in that place were terrified.

The tiring raid was a raid that continued for a very long time. Since the people in the air raid shelters had nothing to eat, no water to drink, and no place to lie down and sleep in, after many hours everybody was very tired.

China had no air defense and could not produce airplanes. All the fighter planes were purchased from abroad. They were second-rate and secondhand planes, and were certainly no match for the Japanese planes. When a Chinese fighter plane came up to fight a Japanese fighter, the Chinese pilot would most likely be shot down and killed. So we nicknamed the Chinese fighter planes "coffins."

If China got money, she could purchase better and more planes in short order. But a pilot cannot be produced overnight. China had only a few well-trained pilots, so the government issued an order that no pilot was allowed to fly a plane to challenge the Japanese fighters. And there was no air defense.

The only air defense China had were the anti-aircraft guns. Since there were not many of them, China used them to protect the war-time capital Chongqing. Then the Chinese set up the air defense of Chongqing by installing an air alarm system. The system had three circles. The first circle was several miles from the city center of Chongqing. When a Japanese airplane touched that circle, a preliminary air alarm would sound. People in the city would know that a Japanese airplane was coming. The second circle was nearer to the city. When the Japanese airplane reached this circle, the second air alarm would sound and people were ready to go to the air shelters. Chongqing was built on a hard-rock hill. Drilling through the rock under the streets would make good shelters. And those shelters were near the stores and easily accessible. The third circle was very close to the city. When the Japanese airplane entered that circle, a third air alarm would sound and everybody must enter the shelters. Bombs would explode in the city.

This air defense system looked good on paper, but it gave the Japanese the opportunity to create the tiring air raid. Knowing that the Chinese fighters would not attack the Japanese bombers, the Japanese sent one bomber at a time and spaced two bombers at exactly the distance between the city and the third circle. When the first bomber finished its bombing and was ready to leave, the second bomber had already reached the third circle. So the air defense team could not relieve the alarm and sound the all clear. People had to stay inside the shelters. The second bomber would be followed by a third bomber in the same way. So the air raid continued for a long time. People in the shelters were prevented from leaving. They were not only tired and hungry, but also out of oxygen.

The ventilation system in the shelters was not adequate. After such a long air raid the shelters no longer had enough fresh air. People were being suffocated. Some tried to get out by force. They were pushed back by guards who were stationed outside the shelters. Some guards even locked the door of a shelter. When the air raid was finally over, the guards opened the door. Only a few people near the door came out. The rest had all been suffocated.

Nobody opened the doors of the stores in the street above the shelters. Those store owners all died in the shelters. This was the largest disaster of an air raid during the full-scale War of Resistance Against Japanese Aggression.

My school, National Central University, was located outside the city of Chongqing. But it was also a target of Japanese bombing. One day about 27 Japanese bombers bombed my university and the surrounding areas. An incendiary bomb fell on my dormitory and burned my mosquito net. There were so many mosquitoes on the campus. You could not sleep without a mosquito net.

Then China realized that she must have airplanes for air defense. So she obtained from the U.S. government a loan to purchase 100 fighter planes, and to hire 100 pilots and a few supporting staff members. The pilots were selected from U.S. Army and Navy Air Forces. As their badge was a tiger with wings, they were nicknamed "Flying Tigers." My life as a "Flying Tiger," who never got off the ground, will be told in the next chapter.

Flying Tigers

The first group of "Flying Tigers" were known as the American Volunteers Group (AVG). I joined AVG in 1941.

AVG was created with a loan that the Chinese government received from the U.S. government. It was part of the Chinese air force, not the American air force. Since the U.S. was not at war with Japan at that time, she could not send her air force to China to fight against the Japanese. That is why those pilots, although they came from the U.S. Army and Navy Air Forces, were called volunteers.

In addition to 100 fighter pilots and Colonel Claire Lee Chennault, Chief of AVG, the staff of AVG included some mechanics, radiomen, intelligence officers, a physician, a nurse, a secretary, and a deputy chief. They were all Americans and needed interpreters. The Chinese Air Force did not have that many interpreters. There were many English-speaking people in China who could qualify as interpreters for AVG, but out of fear that some Japanese spies could penetrate into

AVG, the Chinese Air Force dared not recruit interpreters by advertising publicly. So the Chinese government issued an order to ask students of the English Departments of five leading universities to volunteer to serve as interpreters for AVG for one year. After one year they could return school to the same class as before. So I volunteered for the second time during the war against Japanese.

Before we joined AVG as interpreters, we received a three-month training. We learned air force terminology. We learned U.S.-China relations. We learned the difference between the English and American languages. And we learned some American slang. But there was one word that we never learned but the Americans, especially the radiomen, used in almost every sentence. That is the four-letter word, f--k. Later, when I worked in AVG headquarters and the radioman called to tell me that there was a message for Colonel Chennault, I had difficulty in understanding him because he used so many f--ks in his speech.

Having completed the training, I was assigned to work as the interpreter-code-man in Colonel Chennault's office. There were eight code-men divided into four two-man teams. Each team worked six-hour shifts and the code room was manned 24 hours a day. We decoded and coded all incoming and outgoing messages. The code was rather simple. Each alphabetic letter was represented by two figures. For example, "45216876345698245532" meant "Japs coming", because 45 represented J, 21 a, 68 p, 76 s, 34 c, and so on. Our code book was changed every three months. I do not think the Japanese ever intercepted our messages nor made sense of them.

The headquarters of AVG was a small building in the airfield of Kunming. It had only four rooms. In Colonel Chennault's room were Chennault himself, his English secretary and his Chinese secretary Colonel Shu Boyan (舒伯炎). Colonel Shu also served as Chief of Interpreters and therefore was my immediate superior. Next to Chennault's room was the code room where the code-men worked. Facing Chennault's room was the room of Deputy Chief of AVG, Captain Green. Next to his room was the sitting room where we received guests.

Chennault parked his car just outside the building. His Chinese driver sat in the car all day long. When a code-man had to go to a radio station to pick up a message, the transportation department would send a car or a jeep with a driver to the headquarters for the code-man to use.

The fighter planes AVG first used were P-40s. They were faster and stronger than the Japanese fighters. Chennault taught AVG pilots how to fight the Japanese fighters. When a P-40 was up in the air, it was very difficult for the Japanese fighter to shoot it down. Most P-40s that were lost were lost on the ground in northern Burma. The air alarm system there was not very efficient. Sometimes the Japanese airplanes would sneak in before P-40s could take off. Then the P-40s on the ground would be destroyed by Japanese bombs.

When we interpreters were being trained in 1941, the Japanese bombed Pearl Harbor. The U.S. declared war against Japan. Then the Chinese government asked the U.S. to send her own air force to replace AVG. Later the U.S. 14th Army Air Force came to China. Then the Chinese and American pilots joined forces to establish the U.S.-China United Air Force. As Chennault assumed leadership of all those forces, and members of those forces also called themselves "Flying Tigers." But they did not receive the Flying Tiger badges as I did.

Later, the headquarters of AVG was moved from Kunming to Chongqing, the wartime capital of China. My one-year volunteer service to the air force came to an end. I could choose to either remain in the air force or return to school. I decided to return to school and continue my education. But my university refused to keep its promise to let me rejoin my original class. I had to study all the courses of the missing year and therefore graduated one year later.

After I graduated from the National Central University in 1944, I entered the Chungking Post-Graduate School of Journalism (CPGSJ). I will write another chapter about the CPGSJ, but let me finish my Flying Tiger story first.

Many years later, when I was working as the Curator-Librarian of the East Asia Collection of the Hoover Institution at Stanford University, Colonel Shu Boyan, my former boss at AVG, came to San Francisco, CA. Chennault had passed away in 1958. I asked Shu whether or not he knew Madame Chennault. He said yes. As a matter of fact, when she came to interview Chennault as a newspaper reporter, the interview was held in Chennault's office where Colonel Shu sat and would help if necessary.

I asked Colonel Shu to do me the favor of writing to Madame Chennault and asking her to give the Hoover Institution her husband's personal archives. He did.

Madame Chennault responded to his letter with a letter directly addressed to me. She told me that she could not give me Chennault's archive because West Point and the National Archives had already asked for it. In comparison with those two, Hoover was ranked a low No. 3. After I received her letter, I immediately sent her a reply. I told her that I had three good reasons to ask for Chennault's archive.

First, I was Chennault's code-man. A lot of his incoming and outgoing messages were decoded and coded by me. So his archive is also my archive. I will take very good care of it. Secondly, the purpose of preserving archives is to make them available to scholars and researchers so that they could write a good book or complete an important research project. The library of West Point, as a military school, is not accessible to scholars and researchers. So they would not make optimal use of Chennault's archive. The National Archives has so many archives and it is difficult for anyone to find a personal archive. I did not mention that Chennault was outranked by many VIPs in the National Archives. The third reason is the most important. Chennault's political rival was "Vinegar Joe", General Joseph Warren Stilwell. Stilwell's archive is in the Hoover Institution. Utilizing this archive, a well-known reporter, Theodore Harold White, edited a best-selling book titled "The Stilwell Papers." In that book, Chennault's image is not very favorable. It is very important for Chennault to have a correct image in history. And it is Madame Chennault's duty to ensure that. I told her that if she gave Chennault's archive to me, I would put it right next to Stilwell's archive. Then scholars and researchers would be able to see the viewpoints of both men. Vinegar Joe's viewpoint would be modified and Chennault's standing would become known and understood.

After a few days I received a phone call from Madame Chennault. She said that she would personally bring her husband's archive to me and would arrive by plane on a specific date and time. She asked me to pick her up at San Francisco airport. A few days later, the Hoover Institution held a press conference to announce the arrival of Chennault's archive. Every year since then, the first person to send me a Christmas card was Madame Chennault, Chen Xiangmei (陈香梅).

Chungking Post-Graduate School
of Journalism (I)

Having graduated from the English Department of the National Central University in 1944, I looked for an opportunity to go abroad for advanced studies. As China was an underdeveloped country, it was important for Chinese students to receive advanced education abroad. For a student of the English language, it was particularly important to have advanced education in English-speaking countries like the United States and the United Kingdom.

To go abroad to study was very expensive. My father could not help me because he was living in Japanese-occupied Shanghai then and had no job. The Chinese government had suspended the scholarship for studying English abroad for many years. The only way a poor student could get the opportunity to go abroad for advanced studies was to pass the examination for diplomats and consular officers, and to work in the Ministry of Foreign Affairs (MFA). After a few years at the MFA, he might have a chance to get an assignment abroad. If he was assigned to a country with an advanced educational system, he could take evening courses and receive an advanced degree. Almost all college graduates with an English major took the MFA examination every year. Since the MFA program had only a few vacancies each year and the number of college graduates was significant, it was very difficult to get into the MFA.

When I graduated from college in 1944, China was still at war with Japan. The Chinese government was weak not only militarily but also in providing and disseminating war information. Generalissimo Chiang Kai-shek instructed Dr. Hollington K. Tong, Deputy Minister of Information of Kuomintang, to strengthen China's "war information service". In order to do so, China needed a number of capable English-speaking information officers. China did not have enough such officers. Dr. Tong decided to recruit and train some.

Dr. Tong was a graduate of the School of Journalism at Columbia University in New York City. The Dean of that school then, Professor Ackerman, happened to be his classmate.

So he went to Columbia to see Dean Ackerman and discussed with him the matter of training information officers. They agreed that, in order to train information officers, a school of journalism should be established in China. Columbia's School of Journalism would provide that school with five professors and Dr. Tong whould provide the students.

In an attempt to find the best English students, Dr. Tong posted in newspapers of Chongqing, Chengdu, and Kunming an announcement which mentioned the following:

1. The new school will be called Chungking Post-Graduate School of Journalism (CPGSJ).
2. It will have American professors.
3. All college graduates can apply for the entrance examination.
4. A total of 30 students will be admitted.
5. The students will graduate in one year.
6. After graduation, the students will work in the

Department of International Information in the Ministry of Information of Kuomintang for one year.

7. After the completion of the one-year service, the top ten graduates will be given a scholarship to receive advanced studies in the U.S.

Those conditions were definitely much better than those offered by the MFA. Dr. Tong had the CPGSJ entrance examination held on the same date as the MFA examination. Almost all the best students majoring in English applied for CPGSJ.

Luckily, I passed the CPGSJ entrance examination and was admitted. The courses of CPGSJ were almost identical to those at Columbia University's School of Journalism. For practice, we published an English weekly called *The Chungking Reporter*. This newspaper was given to all foreign correspondents in China then and was sent to the U.S. Library of Congress, members of the U.S. Congress, and many high-ranking American government officials. It did not win the Pulitzer Prize, but it performed an international information service for China during the war.

Chungking Post-Graduate School
of Journalism (II)

B efore the Chungking Post-Graduate School of Journalism was established, it was affiliated to the National Political University (NPU). It had to be so, because by the Chinese law of education then, a graduate school could not be independent. It must belong to a university. So we became part of the NPU. But the CPGSJ, located in the city of Chongqing, was physically quite far from the NPU, located in the village of Nanwenquan (南温泉). And it was administratively and financially quite independent from the NPU. The Alumni Association of NPU in the U.S. considered us as its members. But we rarely attended their meetings.

When the CPGSJ was first established, Columbia's School of Journalism sent five professors to CPGSJ, including the Dean, Dr. Hollington K. Tong being the Chinese Dean and Zeng Xubai (曾虚白) being the Vice Dean. There were three Chinese faculty members. Ma Xingye (马星野), Chairman of the Department of Journalism of the NPU, taught us Chinese journalism. Gan Naiguang (甘乃光), Vice Minister of Foreign

Affairs, taught us international relations. And Pan Gongzhan (潘公展), Member of the Standing Executive Committee of Kuomintang, taught us party principles, a course required for all college students. During the second year of the CPGSJ, the American Dean returned to the U.S. Rodney Gilbert, a veteran China correspondent of an American newspaper became the new Dean. And Columbia University sent an additional assistant professor to CPGSJ.

So we 30 students had six professors. Each professor took care of five students. Every morning class began at 9 a.m. Each student would be given an assignment. The assignments included interviewing newsworthy persons, participating in public activities, investigating social or political cases, and listening to speeches by some VIPs or famous people. As soon as we received our assignments, we left school to do our work. When we complete the ground work, we rushed back to write our reports. We were required to hand in our reports to our advising professors before 5 p.m. The professors would not accept our reports even one minute after 5 p.m. A deadline is a deadline. If a student could not meet the deadline, he would get a "0" for his report. After the professor received the reports, he would ask each individual student to sit next to him and observe all the corrections he made on the report. He graded the report in accordance with the corrections he made.

For practice, we published an English weekly called *The Chungking Reporter*. Good reports could be included in that weekly. We did not make many interesting reports. But one report did make an impact on the Chinese government. China never had a press law but the Chinese government intended to make one. Before the press law was announced, one of my classmates uncovered the provisions of the law and published them in *The Chungking Reporter*. The foreign correspondents in China were shocked to see the law because it seriously limited the freedom of the press. Some provisions might be necessary during the war, but they would not be acceptable in peacetime. So the foreign correspondents protested to the Chinese government and as a result, the press law was never published.

War was not all war. For a long time there was no serious fighting in the China theater during World War II. The life of war correspondents in China became very boring. To relieve them from boredom, Jimmy Wei, a commissioner of the International Department of the Ministry of Information, and a very clever person, suddenly made an announcement. He told the war correspondents that in China, on the 5th day of the 5th month of the lunar calendar, you could stand an egg upright in its shell. And he said that he would demonstrate it on that date. All the war correspondents came to see his demonstration. In no time, he placed not one, but several eggs upright on the cement ground. All war correspondents were surprised and sent out their reports. This became one of the most communicated news stories during WWII.

Actually, this is no trick. An egg can stand upright on almost any surface if it is not too smooth. Try it.

The End of the War

Graduated from the Chungking Post-Graduate School of Journalism (CPGSJ), I had a two-week vacation. My brother David was then working in the city of Xi'an as Captain of General Hu Zongnan's Plain Clothes Team. I went to see him in Xi'an immediately after graduation and stayed in his barracks. One night, I was awakened by fireworks and loud noise in the streets. People were celebrating the surrender of Japan and the end of the War of Resistance Against Japanese Aggression or *Kang Zhan.*

Kang Zhan is the most important event in the history of modern China. More than 20 million Chinese moved from the Japanese-occupied areas along the coast to inland China, which was much less developed than the coastal regions. China was unified during the war. For the first time in their lives, many people living inland realized that Japan was a nation and so was China, and that it was their duty to defend China. The War was very educational to them.

I cut short my vacation and rushed back to CPGSJ to wait for my assignment. The U.S. Marines had already landed in Northern China to help China accept the Japanese surrender and disarm the Japanese troops. Some war correspondents came with the American troops. China needed Public Relations Officers (PRO) to take care of those foreign war correspondents.

The office of PRO was unknown to the Chinese government then. China had Departments of Foreign Affairs in many governmental agencies. China also had Liaison officers. But China never had any PRO. When the American Ambassador telephoned Generalissimo Chiang Kai-shek and asked whether or not China had PRO, not to disappoint the Ambassador, Chiang immediately said yes, although he may not have known what PRO meant. After the phone call, Chiang immediately called the Minister of Information of Kuomintang and asked the Minister if he had any PRO. The Minister immediately answered yes.

In turn, he called the Deputy Minister of Information, Dr. Hollington K. Tong, and asked the latter for PRO. Dr. Tong called the Director of the Bureau of International Information, Mr. Zeng Xubai, who was Vice Dean of the CPGSJ, and asked him to select some graduates of the CPGSJ to serve as PRO.

So Mr. Zeng called five of us to his office and told us that we had been selected as PRO and must go to Northern China immediately. One of us would go to the seaport of Qingdao which was the headquarters of the U.S. 7th Fleet. Two of us were to be stationed in Tianjin where the U.S. Marines landed. One was assigned to the Northeast (Manchuria), but he could not go there because the Russian troops were still present. I was assigned to Beijing, which was called Peiping at that time. Peiping was Generalissimo Chiang's Northern China headquarters and also the headquarters of General Jones, Head of the U.S. Marines in China.

I stayed in Peking Hotel, which was originally a French hotel with a French name. Its dining room served only French food.

My room was No. 319, which was the largest room in the hotel. It was the room of the Japanese Manager during the Japanese occupation of Peiping. I was given two additional rooms in the hotel that I could give to any war correspondent who needed a room. I also had three rooms in another hotel nearby.

I could arrange an appointment for any war correspondent who wanted to interview any person. The highest authority in Peiping then was General Li Zongren (李宗仁), Director of Generalissimo's headquarters. I took a war correspondent to see him. As a former warlord in Guangxi Province, he had a large number of troops under his command, but his troops were not in Peiping then. Peiping was protected by the 34th Army Group, which were General Hu Zongnan's troops. Later, Li became the Acting President of China. But Generalissimo never gave up his control of the government, including the military forces and the treasury. When the Chinese Communists took over the mainland of China, Li exiled himself to the U.S. Later, he returned to China.

Most foreign correspondents in Peiping were experienced reporters. They did not need much help from me. I stayed in my hotel room most of the time and read books. One day I went downstairs to see what the hotel had for sale in its store. Behind the Information Desk I saw a sign that had "PRO" written above a door. I was puzzled because I knew there was no Public Relations Officer in that hotel except me. So I asked the clerk who occupied that room. The clerk hushed me and whispered to me, "That is the place where American soldiers entertain prostitutes."

Marshall's Mission

The end of *Kang Zhan* was the beginning of *Nei Zhan* (Civil War, 内战). Kuomintang began a full-scale civil war throughout the country. Generalissimo Chiang Kai-shek issued an order to the Japanese troops to surrender only to the Kuomintang troops. But the Communists accepted the Japanese surrender anyway.

The Kuomintang troops could not reach many cities in Northern China because the Communists blocked the railroads. American airplanes were used to transport Kuomintang troops to a few major cities in Northern China, but the number of troops that could be transported by plane was quite limited. The only Kuomintang troops that reached Peiping by air was the crack division of General Hu Zongnan—the 34th Group Army.

General Hu's Chief of G-2, Colonel Liu Xiangjie came to Peiping one day. I asked him what his missions were. He said his most important mission was to recruit the troops of the puppet Nanking government. The puppet government was supported by the Japanese during the war. When the Japanese surrendered, the puppet government collapsed and its troops became masterless and got no pay. There were a large number of such troops. Both Kuomintang and Communists needed them. Kuomintang tried to win them over by paying them and giving their commanders a high rank. Colonel Liu's mission was to give pro-Kuomintang puppet commanders high military ranks. Although he was only a colonel himself, he was authorized by Kuomintang government to give a puppet troop commander the rank of major general which was normally the rank of a division chief.

Kuomintang used puppet troops to fight the civil war. There were battles all over the country. U.S. President Harry S. Truman decided to send General George Catlett Marshall to China to establish a truce between Kuomintang and the Communists. Thus began Marshall's Mission.

The Mission started by organizing a Committee of Three, composed of Marshall, General Zhang Qun (张群), who was later replaced by Zhang Zhizhong (张治中), representing Kuomintang and Zhou Enlai (周恩来) to represent the Communists. The Committee reached a truce agreement and established a Truce Executive Headquarters (TEH) at the Union Hospital in Peiping. The TEH had field stations in several places. Whenever and wherever a battle happened, the TEH would send a team to enforce the truce. The TEH sent supplies to all field stations by airplane once a week. Foreign correspondents could use that airplane to visit the battlefields and collect news.

Once a correspondent of the French newspaper *Le Figaro* in Paris wanted to interview General Nie Rongzhen (聂荣臻) in Zhangjiakou. I went with him. Nie once studied in France. The correspondent spoke French to General Nie and Nie responded in French. The two spoke French all throughout the interview. That left me out completely because I did not understand French.

Nie hosted us in a hotel built by the Japanese outside the city of Zhangjiakou. When we got up the next morning, I asked the correspondent how well he slept. He said he did not sleep at all. Something was biting him all night. It was bed bugs. He never had them in Peiping or Paris.

Zhangjiakou was then the largest city controlled by the Communists in China. I saw a number of Communist soldiers in the city. They carried all kinds of rifles, made by the Germans in Shandong, made in Japan, and made in various provinces of China. Some of those rifles were so poorly made that the barrel would become so hot after ten shots that you could not hold it. But the soldiers looked quite healthy—healthier than Kuomintang soldiers.

In Zhangjiakou, I met the well-known female writer Ding Ling (丁玲) and writer Zhou Erfu (周而复). They probably worked for the Chinese daily *ZINCHAGI RHBAO* (《晋察冀日报》). They gave me several latest issues of the paper. I saw a story of the

Communist soldiers standing on the seashores of Shandong Province waiting for the landing of American troops of the 9th Army under the command of General Stilwell. They knew General Stilwell would give them American-made equipment. But they waited in vain because the Japanese surrendered before General Stilwell could land.

On my flight back from Zhangjiakou to Peiping, the airplane tried to make a stop at Kweisui (归绥, now Hohhot). As the pilot prepared for landing, he suddenly realized that the runway was too short. He had to pull up the airplane immediately before it would crash. Luckily, there was no building beyond the end of the runway, only flat desert. The airplane was able to glide above the desert and fly upwards. I avoided becoming a casualty of war.

As the civil war spread to Manchuria, the TEH established a branch in the city of Changchun in Jilin Province. I was invited by TEH to serve as the Head of the Press Section of its Changchun Branch. Changchun (Hsinking) was the capital of "Manchukuo", the puppet regime established by the Japanese after their occupation of Manchuria in 1931. Puyi was the Emperor of "Manchukuo". The Japanese tried to build a palace for him, but the war ended before the palace was built. Only its foundation had been completed when the Japanese surrendered. Later, a well-known Chinese architect, Liang Sicheng, built a house on that foundation. The house was later used by the Institute of Geology of Changchun.

At that time, the top commander of the Communist troops in Manchuria was Lin Biao (林彪). Some foreign correspondents wanted to interview him. So I arranged an airplane to take them to Harbin. As the flight was about to take off, a reporter of the newspaper *Ta Kung Pao* approached me and asked me to let him go to Harbin, too. Since there was no vacant seat on the airplane, I let him have my seat. He was very grateful. But I missed the chance of meeting Lin Biao in person.

The top political leader of the Communists in Manchuria then was Li Minran (李敏然). Not many people knew his background. Actually, he was once Head of the Communist Party of China, Li Lisan (李立三). After he lost his position as the party chief, he exiled himself in the Soviet Union. He probably returned to China with the Soviet troops.

Since both Kuomintang and the Communists thought that they could win the civil war, enforcement of the truce was very difficult. The Kuomintang troops, mainly the New First and New Sixth Armies trained by General Joseph Stilwell, succeeded in taking Changchun and even established a beachhead on the northern shore of the Songhua River. But they could not advance further northwards to Harbin because they were outnumbered by the Communists.

One day, the Governor of Jilin Province, General Liang Huasheng (梁华盛), gave me a banquet. Around the table of ten people I saw quite a few wearing the insignia of *junzhang* (军长, Commander of an Army). I knew there were only two Armies around Changchun—New First Army and New Sixth Army. And I knew their commanders were Generals Zheng Dongguo (郑洞国) of the New First Army and Liao Yaoxiang (廖耀湘) of the New Sixth Army. I asked them how there could be so many Army Commanders. They all laughed. They told me that in order to fool the Communists, they raised the rank of all the Division Commanders to that of Army Commander. There were three Divisions in each Army so there were eight Army Commanders, instead of two. They thought that the Communists might be led into believing that Kuomintang had more troops than they actually had. There is a well-known Chinese saying, "兵不厌诈 (there can never be too much deception in war)." Those smart soldiers had put this idea into practice.

When I was in Changchun, President Truman sent his personal representative Edwin Wendell Pauley to Manchuria to investigate how much damage the Soviet occupation of Manchuria had done to the industrial economy, including the removal and destruction of industrial equipment, and pillage. I accompanied Pauley's mission to inspect several factories and the huge Xiaofengman (小丰满) hydroelectric power plant which supplied electricity to almost all major cities in Manchuria. In his report to President Truman, Pauley estimated the damage at U.S. $2 billion.

As I completed my tenure at the Changchun Branch of TEH, I returned to my job as a PRO of the Chinese government in Peiping. Not long after that the truce between Kuomintang and the Communists was irretrievably broken. And Marshall's Mission failed. He returned to the U.S. and I returned to Nanjing. The International Department of the Kuomintang Ministry of Information had become the Government Information Office of the Executive Council and its headquarters had moved from Chongqing to Nanjing. According to the advertisement of the Chungking Post-

Graduate School of Journalism, after graduation we had to serve for only one year at the International Department of the Central Ministry of Information. And the top ten graduates would be given a scholarship to study in the U.S. I had worked for the International Department more than one year. And I was one of the top ten graduates. So I returned to Nanjing in 1947 to await the scholarship.

今年九十七，是大利大吉。

儿女都孝顺，都很有出息。

约我欧陆游，送我还故里。

故国有朋友，故乡有亲戚。

热情又好客，接待很得体。

后接P119

Leaving China

While waiting for a scholarship in Nanjing in 1947, Soong Tzu-wen (宋子文) was the Premier. The Chinese government was in serious shortage of foreign exchange. So Tzu-wen issued an order which stated that no one was allowed to receive a grant of more than $2,000 in foreign exchange without his personal approval. My scholarship was $3,500. The total amount of scholarships for the ten of us was therefore $35,000. If Tzu-wen did not approve it, our dream of going to the U.S. would evaporate. We waited and waited for his approval, but heard nothing for a long time.

One day we mentioned this to the American advisor who was working in the Government Information Office. We told him about the advertisement of the Chungking Post-Graduate School of Journalism in which the Chinese government promised to give us a scholarship after the completion of service and about Soong Tzu-wen's order which annulled our scholarship. The American advisor was surprised to learn that the Chinese government did not keep its promise. He told us that Madame Chiang Kai-shek was going to give foreign advisors a banquet that night and he was going to see her. He would tell Madame Chiang, Soong Mei-ling, sister of Soong Tzu-wen, about this.

The next morning we received a phone call from the Bank of China in Shanghai, telling us that there were ten $3,500 checks in the bank waiting for us to pick up. That showed how efficient Madame Chiang could be.

Madame Chiang not only secured the scholarship money for us—she also wanted to teach us the American way of life. She asked her capable assistant General Huang Renlin (黄仁霖) to give us a dinner in order to teach us table manners. Huang took us to a Western-style restaurant and ordered fried chicken for us. We had to use fork and knife to eat. One of us, while cutting the chicken, managed to launch a piece of chicken across the table and hit a person on the other side. The fried chicken became a flying chicken.

So we all received our checks. And those checks were so good that they could be cashed anywhere in China. China was then suffering from serious inflation and $3,500 could buy a lot of things. One of us decided not to go to the U.S. but to invest the money in business. He made a small fortune.

For those of us who wanted to go to the U.S., our problem was to get an American visa from the American Consulate-General. In order to prevent people with tuberculosis from entering the U.S., the American Consulate required every visa applicant to present an X-ray picture. I had pleurisy during my time at Graduate School and feared that an X-ray might show a scar on my lungs. So I hesitated to take an X-ray picture. Mr. Xiong Xianghui (熊向晖), a good friend of mine, was also applying for visa then. He was about the same size as me and volunteered to take an X-ray in my name and gave it to me. So I obtained a visa with his X-ray.

Both he and my brother David served as General Hu Zongnan's aide-de-camp during the war. General Hu gave each of them a scholarship of $1,800 to go to the U.S. to study. The three of us left China for the U.S. on the same ship in the summer of 1947. David and I went to the University of Wisconsin, and Xiong to the Western Reserve University in Cleveland. Thus began my exile in the U.S. and my good-bye to China.

前言

非富即贵，不是要人就是名人——这样的人才会出版自传。我跟他们都不沾边，我是应孩子们的请求写了这本自传。他们很棒，我爱他们。

我于中国农历 1920 年 2 月 22 日出生在浙江温州。当时的中国，积贫积弱。天灾人祸，外敌入侵和内战，贫穷愚昧，饥饿和社会不公，构成了老百姓的日常生活。

那时，如果有人在成长过程中没有挨过饿，他是幸运的；如果没有被盗抢过，他是幸运的；如果没有被坑蒙拐骗过，他非常幸运；如果可以去上学并通过所有重要的考试，他非常幸运；如果交有挚友，他是幸运的；如果有父母的疼爱，他是幸运的；如果子女孝顺，他是幸运的。我是一个非常非常幸运的人。

温州是个生活的好地方。"温"代表温暖,"州"代表地方。因此,温州气候温暖,冬暖夏凉。一年到头,也就下一两次雪。雪不黏,不适合堆雪人。

马氏家族

　　我是我父亲的第二个儿子。我父亲是我爷爷的第二个儿子。我爷爷是我太爷爷的第二个儿子。爷爷有四个兄弟和一个妹妹。父亲也是有四个兄弟和一个妹妹。我亦有四个兄弟和一个妹妹。传承这样的家庭传统——次子，有五子一女——可能很难。我未能沿袭这个传统，膝下一子二女，不过于我而言他们都很棒。

　　马家是温州的名门望族。我们不是最富最贵的，却以书香门第和艺术传统而闻名，温州的其他家族无法比拟。

　　我的先祖五代前是解元，他开创了马家的书香传统。解元是乡试（省考）的第一名。过去在中国，每三年全国各个不同的行政区域都要举行科举考试。通过考试的前100名有不同的称谓。通过院试的叫秀才，通过乡试的叫举人，举人里的第一名就叫解元。我的先祖中了解元，同一年，他的兄弟也通过考试，中了举人。

解元府

学子一旦考取功名，政府往往会赏赐给他土地，以资薪俸。受赏者可以把土地出租，以租金为生。功名越高，薪俸就越高；薪俸越高，收入就越多。两兄弟分别中了解元和举人，就有足够的钱财在温州城里盖两座大宅子。宅子紧挨着，几乎占了温州城里的半个街区。

解元的宅子叫解元府，解元府的大门上横挂着一块大匾额，上书"解元"二字。我就出生在这座解元府里。

我祖父家里几乎所有的成员，还有他四个兄弟的家庭成员，都住在解元府里，因为他们都是解元的后代。这座宅第有时住户多达30人，其中有10来个孩子和我年龄相仿。在马氏家族里，我要找玩伴很容易。所以我从不在大街上和陌生人玩。我的玩伴都是家人，所以在我幼稚的心灵中，四海之内皆兄弟。

解元府最深处的庭院是我父亲马公愚和伯父马孟容练习书法及画画的地方。孩提时，我就喜欢看他们挥毫作画。我自己也爱上了画画，在同龄人中我算是画得很好的。

那时中国国力衰弱，西方列强正在蚕食中国。父亲非常爱国，他并不鼓励我成为画家。他说："书画救不了国。年轻人应该学习科学与技术，科技兴国。"他同时指出了学问对艺术的重要性。他跟我说："长大以后，如果你有好学问，同时还是个好画家，人们就会尊称你为画家；如果只会作画而学问不好，充其量只能算是个画匠而已。"画匠和画家的社会地位不可相提并论。如此这般，我年少时当画家的梦想就被父亲扼杀在萌芽状态。打那之后，家里的浴室就是我被允许涂画的唯一的地方。后来我们家里要加一层新油漆，母亲觉得我的艺术水平不太高，也只让我漆客人很少看到的浴室。

我在高中时进了省立上海中学的理科。省立上海中学是当时中国最好的中学。学生毕业后，都能顺利通过中国任何一所好大学的入学考试。如果我从那里毕业，可以去上最好的理工科大学，将来有一天能当个顶尖的科学家。但我却没能读完高中。1937年，日本人侵略华北，全面抗战爆发。我牢记年轻时父亲对我的教诲：人的一生中，救国比追求个人情趣更重要。于是我在高中二年级念完后，就投笔从戎，志愿参加抗战。1938年夏天，我离开上海到陕西去参军，父亲给了我90块袁大头（银元）。战争初期，通货膨胀严重，军队和政府公职人员降薪，90块银元可能超过一个将军一年的薪俸。

　　我的童年是幸运而快乐的。父母不仅和蔼可亲，而且都受过良好的教育。

　　20世纪早期，政府为推动国家现代化，在每个省都设有一所"洋学堂"。之所以称作"洋学堂"，是因为和传统学堂教授四书五经不同，这些学校教的都是西方国家的课程。学校的多数老师都是西方人，往往是英美大学的教授。学生们学习英语、数学、物理和化学等科目。

　　浙江省的洋学堂设在省会杭州。我父亲和我大伯都去了那个洋学堂学习——父亲主修英语，大伯主修数学。这恐怕是当时中国学生所能接受的最好的教育。

　　我母亲也受到了当时最好的女子教育。在旧中国，女孩子受教育的唯一方式就是家里聘请私塾先生来教，只有富裕的家庭才能这么做。有些富人家会允许他们的穷亲戚或朋友的女儿受教于同一个私塾先生。那时没有公立女学校。我的母亲很幸运，在她到了学龄之际，温州有了第一所公立女校。

她上了学，并在班上名列第一。作为温州第一所女校的第一名毕业生，她声名鹊起。

母亲之所以出众还有另一个原因。在她那个年代，女孩子从小就要缠足。她们被告知，如果不缠足，将来会找不到好丈夫。不过母亲受过现代教育，她拒绝缠足。因此，她成了温州同龄人中唯一一个不缠足的女孩。她便以一位女性革命者而闻名。

母亲嫁给父亲时，父亲已是有名的书法家，但我母亲更有名。我的父母都受过良好的教育，他们对我很好，给了我幸福和健康的童年。只要市场上有儿童杂志，父亲就给我订阅。我有自己的书柜，里面放着满满的儿童图书，还有许多体育用品。

一起住在解元府里的堂兄妹和小叔们，经常会来我这儿借阅图书杂志。看来，我命中注定要成为图书管理员。

儿童教育

　　母亲是我儿童时代主要的启蒙老师。她会时不时给我讲些古典谚语和格言，指导我的言行举止。比如，了解到我很少做家庭作业，她就会举"少壮不努力，老大徒伤悲"之类的谚语，跟我强调用功学习和勤奋努力的重要性。

　　上小学时，我真的不怎么做家庭作业。那是因为没必要做。我读过很多儿童图书，定期阅读好的儿童杂志，积累了大量的基础知识，应付小学考试绰绰有余。我从来不用临考前死记硬背，也从未考试不及格，甚至成绩不错。

　　儿童教育包括正规学校教育，从幼儿园开始。在我小时候，温州只有一所幼儿园，还是浙江省政府教育厅资助成立的。幼儿园隶属于省立小学，只有一个房间，可容纳 20 个孩子。温州那时约有 200 万人口，每个孩子都想上幼儿园。上幼儿园必须考试，相当于我们现在的智力测验。名额有限而报名者众多，录取率恐怕是世界上最低的。

我5岁时，母亲带我到幼儿园参加入学考试。园子里到处都是孩子，人头攒动。所有孩子要考完试，恐怕得花几天工夫。我运气好，当天就参加了考试。考官坐在我对面一张小桌子后，要我做些傻傻的事情，如玩弹子游戏、画画、复述数字、看图识物等。

几天后，幼儿园发布录取公告，我名列榜首。

在中国，从幼儿园到小学，从小学到初中，从初中到高中，从高中到大学，从大学到读研究生，每一层级的教育都有入学考试。幸运之神总在入学考试中关照我，我没有一次入学考试不是顺利通过。

但我并不是总能在学校取得好成绩，我也不总是用功学习。研究生阶段是个例外，那时，我在为获得赴美留学的奖学金而勤奋刻苦着。我一直记得母亲对我的教诲："少壮不努力，老大徒伤悲。"我虽已到鲐背之年，但并不伤悲。我非常幸运，有三个非常勤奋而且孝顺的子女，他们不让我"老大徒伤悲"。

天天讲故事，常常吃酒席。

我的身体好，补品也不必。

平地多走路，大厦有电梯。

只要不摔跤，没病不求医。

后接 P175

119

择友

从加利福尼亚州阿拉梅达我公寓的阳台望出去，可以看到马路对面的鸟类禁猎区。那里栖息着各种各样的鸟儿，有黑的，有白的，但它们从不混杂在一起。这恰恰印证了英文中的一句谚语，"Birds of a feather flock together（同一种羽毛的鸟结伴而行）"。中国也有"物以类聚"的谚语，说的是同样的意思。中国人用它来教育孩子如何择友。择友是教育上最重要的问题之一，因为孩子们会从朋友那里学到许多东西。我上初中时的亲身经历就是这种影响的明证。

1932年，我开始上初中一年级第一学期，依旧沿袭小学时的坏习惯，不做家庭作业，在体育和游戏上花了不少时间。我有一个好朋友，来自本省一个不发达的地区，从未见识过温州这个既大又摩登的城市。他对城里很多东西都觉得新鲜，喜欢到处看看，体验体验。他经常要我跟他一起去，一起玩。我逃了很多课，结果最重要的课程里，英语和数学这两门不及格。那个学期我留级了。

母亲发现我成绩掉队的原因后，就去找我的同班同学曾守中。他是一个好学生。小时候，他家境殷实。后来他父亲骤然去世，他知道，将来有一天他得撑起这个家，于是变得成熟，刻苦学习，不浪费时间，也不乱花钱。他父亲去世后，他住到了我母亲的一个远房亲戚家。有一天，母亲带我到她这个亲戚家串门，遇到了守中。母亲要他和我做朋友，守中答应了。从那时开始，我大部分时间就和守中在一起。我们一起学习，一起玩耍。我的成绩上去了，顺利通过所有考试。到了初中三年级，也就是最后一年，我成了全班唯一的三优生——学习、体育和品行三科全优。

　　毕业后，我和三个同学一起去上海，参加省立上海中学的入学考试。那是当时中国最难考进的学校。我是那年唯一被录取的温州学生。感谢守中，我从黑鸟变成了白鸟。

支离东北风尘际
漂泊西南天地间
三峡楼台淹日月
五溪衣服共云山
羯胡事主终无赖
词客哀时且未还
庾信平生最萧瑟
暮年诗赋动江关

抄杜甫咏怀古迹五首之一 作者手书

战争

　　抵抗日寇侵略的战争，也叫"抗日战争"，或简称"抗战"，可以说是现代中国历史上最重大的事件。抗战历经 14 年，持续时间比第二次世界大战长 8 年，伤亡人数超过了整个二战，影响到几乎每一个中国人的生活，当然包括我在内。

　　1937 年全面抗战爆发时，我还在省立上海中学读书。战争使我想当一名科学家的梦想破灭了。

　　日本军阀野心勃勃，企图征服整个世界。要征服世界，必先征服中国。1931 年，日本人发动了"九一八事变"，占领了中国的东北。1937 年，日军企图跨过卢沟桥，进入北平城。中国军队奋起抵抗，全面战争爆发。

　　中国政府知道日本迟早要侵略中国。为准备应对日军迫在眉睫的入侵，政府下令完成第一学年学业的高中学生必须接受为期 3 个月的军事训练。"卢沟桥事变"爆发时，我正在当时江苏的省会镇江受训。训练我们的军官来自第八十八师——中国一支精锐的国防师。

每天早晨，主管训练营日常事务的旅长主持晨训，并作简短讲话。有一天，他没有露面。后来我才知道他去了上海，视察那里的阵地。因为日本已经开始运兵到上海了。

当时，我是直接从省立上海中学去镇江受训的，行李都留在学校。过了几个月回到上海后，我就不能去学校取行李了，因为学校在中国地界，而我家在法租界。战事把所有外国租界通往中国地界的道路都阻断了。结果，我丢了所有的行李，包括我最珍爱的网球拍。后来，日本人把我的学校变成了一座军营。我不知道是哪个幸运的日本兵拿了我的网球拍。

日本人占领省立上海中学后，我变得无学可上。于是我回到温州，继续在温州中学求学。不久，位于法租界的上海美专腾出教室，让省立上海中学的学生上午用。我便回到上海，继续上学。

中国军队撤离上海时，有意在公共租界北面苏州河边上的四行仓库大楼留下一个营的兵力，以迟滞日军对首都南京的进攻。这个营就是后来著名的"八百壮士"。实际上，军队营的标准建制为 400 人，而不是 800 人。为壮大声势，该营自称一个团，中国政府将这个营的营长军衔提升为团长，他就是谢晋元。谢死后葬在上海，我父亲为他撰写了碑文。

战前我在镇江军训时，谢晋元是我的团长。他率领部队在那幢大楼里顽强抵抗日军进攻，有些炮弹落在公共租界。为了确保租界居民的安全，公共租界当局和日军展开谈判，要求谢部解除武装，转移到公共租界内。谢部被安置在公共租界内的一幢旧营房里，外面由外国军队把守。我和我的同班同学都是谢军训时的兵，每个周末都会去看他，给他和他的兵带些食物和需要的物品。

我们也做些其他爱国和抗日的事情，这自然激怒了日本人。但他们不能派兵进入公共租界，于是就开始搞绑架。有一天，报纸报道日本人绑架了一名中国学生，把他弄到了日租界。这件事让父亲很担心，他对我说，如果我想继续留在上海完成学业，最好当一个顺民，如果我想离开上海，就会当难民。我对父亲说，我既不想当顺民也不想当难民，我想当兵。

到
第
一
军
去

　　1938 年的一天，一个叫黄诵和的年轻人来到我家。他说
自己从内地来，带来了我哥马大恢的消息。战争爆发前，马
大恢在天津南开大学读书。南开大学和北京大学及清华大学
的学生计划要迁到云南省的昆明，组建西南联合大学。在西
去昆明的路上，很多学生滞留在长沙，组成了长沙临时大学。
许多年轻人为战争出力都自愿参军，或组织战地服务团。长
沙临时大学的一些学生也组织了战地服务团，准备开赴前线
去。马大恢就是其中一员。

　　那时，胡宗南将军指挥下的第一军，已经从上海撤到了
武汉。得知长沙临时大学的学生组建了一个战地服务团，他
就想让这个服务团加入第一军。他向长沙派了个年轻的湖南
籍军官去见战地服务团的领导们，劝说他们去武汉见胡宗南
将军。年轻的军官不辱使命。那个战地服务团后来去了武汉，
见到了胡将军。

　　在武汉，胡宗南告诉他们，第一军将移师陕西省，总部

在西安。战地服务团将改名为第一军随军服务团（下文简称"服务团"），主要任务是帮助动员人民参加抗战，并对当地官员和师资进行教育培训。服务团分成几个小组，每一组负责培训一个村。随军服务团总部设在凤翔县。服务团领导直接对胡将军负责。地方和军队官员都很配合服务团的工作。黄告诉我们，我哥马大恢身体健康，工作出色。全家人听到这个消息都很高兴。

黄准备几天后返回第一军。这是我参军的绝好机会。于是，我向父亲提出，要和黄一起去看马大恢并到第一军当兵。父亲欣然同意了我的请求。我准备踏上漫长的旅途。

离家

在和黄去内地之前，我从来没有离开过东南沿海地区。我对外面的世界几乎一无所知。黄是大学生，我父母信任他，相信他会一路照顾我。

从上海去内地，首先要坐船到香港。当时在上海的人都想离开，要弄到船票不容易。每一艘轮船的舱位都是超额预订，几乎所有的乘客都去内地，所以这种船也被称作"难民船"。

黄有两个女性朋友要跟他一起赴内地。一个和我一样，想去第一军当兵，另一个只是去看看朋友。幸运的是，我们四个人都买到了票，一起登船。

登船以后，我们发现所有的房间都已经有人占用了。要两天时间才能抵达香港。我们只能在甲板上找可以睡下的地方。我们找了很久，好不容易找到一块可以放下两张军毯的地方。我们就让两位女学生睡在一张军毯里，我同黄睡在另一张军毯里。

　　船沿着黄浦江朝东海驶去，经过一艘停泊在日租界附近江面上的日本军舰。日本人命令所有过往的商船都挂上布幕，不让旅客看到军舰上的枪炮。其实这是多此一举，因为自从1937年起，这艘军舰就一直停泊在那里。上海所有的人都见过。

　　经过两天两夜的航行，我们终于抵达香港。倚在轮船栏杆上，欣赏着维多利亚港的美景，我问同行的一位女孩在上海上的哪所学校，她说是务本女中。我再问她和黄是怎么认识的，她说黄是她的同学。我问她，黄怎么可以在女中上学呢？她反问我："难道你不知道黄是女子吗？"我说不知道，她们都笑了。我和一个女孩子同毯共眠了两夜，竟然不知道她是女儿身！她们要求我看看黄的喉咙，问道："你看到她的喉咙有像骨头一样突出的肿块吗？"我说没有。她们说："女孩的喉咙是平的，男孩才有喉结。"这是我离家后上的第一课，就是学会怎样区分男女。

战时旅行

在香港下船后，我们立即搭乘另一艘轮船前往广州。抵达广州港后，我们叫了一辆出租车去火车站，准备购买前往内地的车票。我们吃惊地发现，火车站的大门洞开，里面空空荡荡，看不到一个人影。我们买不到票，但车站里停着一列火车。于是我们就爬了进去，找到座位坐下来，休息。

约摸过了半个钟头，许多人走进车站。他们惊讶地发现车上竟然还坐了我们四个人。原来我们进站时，刚好碰上一场空袭。日机正在轰炸广州，人们都往防空洞里躲避，可我们却毫无所知，就这样在火车上等待。幸运的是，日本人并没有轰炸火车站。不然，我们早就成了战争的牺牲品。

为躲避日军轰炸，火车昼伏夜行。火车上没有餐车，也不卖任何食品。火车抵达村镇车站时，小商贩们纷纷聚集在车厢窗户外，向我们兜售各式各样的食品。商贩都是些贫苦的农民和他们的妻儿，衣衫褴褛，手脏兮兮的。作为从上海来，除了母亲做的饭菜从没吃过其他食品的我，自然接受不了这些人兜售的东西。

　　火车到达第一站长沙要行驶两天两夜，路上总得吃点什么。我发现沿途有一些农民在兜售荔枝和龙眼。这些带壳的水果倒是干净的。于是我买了几盒，一路上就靠它们充饥。整整两天两夜，我的肚子里没有淀粉，却填满了大量的维生素 C。

在长沙

我们去陕西省第一军驻地途中，之所以要在长沙停留，是因为服务团的两个成员此时正在长沙休探亲假。他们想让我们长途跋涉去陕西前在他们家歇息几天。

他们的房子在长沙城中心。就在我们抵达长沙的那一天，日军飞机轰炸了长沙火车东站。长沙城没有空防。朋友担心我们丧生于敌机轰炸之中，于是领着我们到了长沙东郊他们在乡下的房子。村庄的名字如同其家族名，叫曹家坪，意思是"曹家的平地"。

显然，朋友家是村子里最大的地主，他们的房子很大。到了不久，他们便热情款待我们，菜品丰盛，色香俱佳。此时我已饥肠辘辘，开饭后就迫不及待地往嘴里夹了一大块鱼。味道有点古怪，完全不同于我以前吃过的鱼。我不敢吞下去，又夹了块猪肉。味道也是怪怪的，和鱼一样辛辣，犹如红辣椒，呛得我舌头发麻，涕泪直流，除了米饭，别的什么也吃不下去。

　　主人这才知道我不能吃辣，但他们也没别的法子。那里所有的菜都是辣的。村子里的商店不卖新鲜食品。村民要买新鲜食品需要碰上赶集的日子，每十天里只有固定的三天。我们在的时候，集市不开，所以在那里的三天，我仅吃白米饭充饥。

　　离家前，我不知辛辣为何物。中国菜有五种口味：甜、酸、苦、辣、咸。温州人不吃辣。作为一个真正的温州人，我也五味不全。

到第一军去
（续）

经过几天休息，我们继续向陕西的第一军行进。胡宗南将军此前已指定凤翔作为随军服务团驻地。凤翔是除了省城西安外陕西最大的县。因为凤翔不通铁路，所以我们无法坐火车去，只能在离它最近的车站下车。车站很小，找不到地方吃饭和歇脚。到了以后，我们决定继续步行去凤翔。

天公不作美。下火车时，我们遇到了倾盆大雨。雨中的黄土变得稀软，道路已成为一条浅溪。每走一步，泥浆都要漫过膝盖，根本不可能走得快。我把行李放到一辆牛车上，那是唯一可行的交通工具。牛走得比我还慢。她十分羸弱，害得我不时要停下来推着车走。从火车站到凤翔城10里（5千米）地，我们几乎走了一整天。

冒雨行军，走这么长的路，到达服务团驻地时，我已经筋疲力尽了。服务团里有两个医生，但没有药。因为担心我会得重感冒，他们烧了开水，放进一些姜和红糖，让我喝姜汤。姜汤很好喝，我喝过后就睡去了。醒来，身体和精神完好如初。

　　我学到了中医上的一课：原来，姜汤加红糖可以预防感冒。

胡宗南将军确定凤翔为服务团的服务区，服务团总部就设在凤翔县城的中心地区，团员们被分别派驻该县不同地方。

服务团的主要任务就是动员民众积极抗战。当地民众的教育水平很低，要让他们明白抗战的意义，费时费力。此类例子不胜枚举。比如说，抗战期间，我们往往用"东洋鬼子"这样的贬义词来称呼日本侵略者。有一个农民就问："我们人怎么能与鬼子（灵魂）作战呢？"另一个农民说："（和日本人）作战是慈禧太后的事，我们干吗要参加？"这说明，要让人们理解抗战，我们得做多少教育启蒙工作呀！

服务团只有 35 个人。这么少的团员要对全县人民进行动员教育是不可能的。于是，我们采取了先让教育者受教育的办法，也就是让这个县的小学老师先接受教育。我们为这些老师开设了几个培训班。在培训完小学老师后，我们再对县里位阶最低的行政官员——保长、甲长们——进行培训，希望以此提高民众的受教育水平。

但我们忽视了一件事。当时内地很多民众都吸鸦片。为遏制鸦片蔓延，政府制定了严格的法律，严禁种植、贩卖和吸食鸦片。种植和贩卖鸦片会被判死刑，吸食鸦片会坐牢。这些法律人尽皆知。

那时的油很贵，所以一到晚上，整个凤翔县城就漆黑一片，路灯不开，门灯不亮。但总有一家店铺门前会亮着灯光，那就是鸦片馆。

发现这一无法容忍的现象时，我们马上报告了胡宗南将军，要求处决鸦片馆的老板和凤翔县县长。胡将军有这个权力，但战时要处决陕西省最大县的县长，兹事体大。他必须找到一个办法，既能让县长活命，同时又能满足我们在报告中提出的要求。

胡将军手下有一些政治官员，充当他政治上的参谋。他本可以派其中一人来和我们谈。但胡将军清楚，他手下的政治顾问根本不是我们这些来自中国最好大学的优秀学生的对手。他需要更好的顾问。最后，他找到了缪凤林——著名历史学家，国立中央大学的教授。他请缪教授来凤翔和我们对话，缪教授同意了。

缪教授来凤翔给我们上了一课。鉴于我们这些志愿者为参军抗战而放弃学业，他一开始先表扬了我们的自我牺牲和爱国精神，然后简要介绍了一番中日关系史以及政府采取的抗战战略。最后，他对我们说，战争代价昂贵，中国政府急需资金将抗战继续到底。陕西没有外贸，工业薄弱，省政府战时的收入只能靠地方税。凤翔作为陕西省最大的县，是纳税大户，该县 80% 的税收恰恰来自那间小鸦片馆。如果把鸦片馆关了，把鸦片馆老板杀了，凤翔对抗战的贡献就会急剧减少。并且，处决鸦片馆老板会对内地鸦片贸易和政府收入造成严重影响，政府抗战恐怕难以为继。缪教授说，有两条路可选，要么关闭鸦片馆、处决县长，要么继续抗战，让我们自己选择。听了这番话，我们无言以对。

　　服务团成员和当地民众建立起了很好的关系。35 个成员被分配到一些村镇。除了正常的教育工作，我们还为当地民众建立了几个卫生站，提供初级医疗服务。我们从第一军得到一些药品，免费发放给贫穷的病人。服务团成员中有两个医生和几个护士。我们把卫生知识融入教育工作中。当地老百姓很感谢我们为他们提供免费医疗服务，对我们很信任。他们知道我们和当地最有权力的政府当局——胡宗南将军——有直接联系，所以会经常要求我们帮着解决一些与政府之间的问题。

　　民众对我们的信任，自然引发了当地官员和第一军政治官员的妒忌。我们直接向胡将军反映民众的疾苦和诉求，侵犯了他们的行政管辖权。一天，我们接到胡将军的电话，要求服务团成员到他所在的西安总部去。

　　胡将军在一个会议室里单独接见我们。他的身边，是一大摞堆得高高的文件。他用手指了指那堆文件，说："这些都是情报官员的报告，他们说你们是共产党。"

这项指控很严重。虽然国共两党那时正在联手抗战，但国民政府和军队里不允许共产党员存在。此外，胡将军对防止年轻人去共产党总部延安参加八路军还负有特殊责任。他自然不能允许自己的军队里有共产党员。

胡将军接着肯定了我们弃学从戎、自愿抗日的行为，说我们都是爱国青年，他不会惩罚我们，而是给了以下三个选择：

一、如果我们想回学校继续读书，他会发给我们旅费并承担学费。如果我们要回家，他也会为我们付旅费。

二、如果我们中间有共产党员想去延安参加八路军，他会指示包围延安的国民党军队一路放行。

三、如果我们想留在第一军，他会开设一期特别培训班，我们受训后就成了胡将军的学生。没有人会说他的学生是共产党。

我们作了选择，会见结束。第一军随军服务团存在9个月后，就此解散。我在第一军的军事生涯也画上了句号。

特别培训班

　　全面抗战期间（1937—1945），政府为训练政治官员，建立了四个战干团（战时工作干部训练团）。其中，第四团在陕西省西安市，在胡宗南将军的管辖下。为了让服务团团员接受特别培训，胡将军在战干团第四团里开设了一个特别班，叫"第四团学员队第三期"。这个班的人叫学员，待遇比普通学生要高。我们有自己的校园和宿舍，不住在战干团第四团的营地。

　　胡将军知道，服务团成员在学生时代受到过共产主义或"左"倾思想的影响，他派了两个有名的前共产党员当我们的教员。他们教授共产主义和中共历史，并讲述了他们在共产党内的亲身经历和中共领导人的一些故事。他们讲的课非常有趣。

　　受训三个月结束后，我们毕了业并被分配到部队从事各种政治工作。我被授予少尉军衔，到国民政府战时北方最高当局——委员长西安行营——政治部第二处工作。第二处的处长杨尔瑛先生是俄国问题专家，讲一口流利的俄语。他给我们讲了抗战初期他为俄国帮助中国抗日的空军飞行员当翻译的经历。他不懂政治工作，却有很好的经商头脑。1949年国民党军队撤退到台湾时，他在台北购置了一幢很大的公寓楼，然后把公寓出租给那些来台人员。公寓楼总是住满了人。他收收租金，发了大财。后来我每次去台湾，他总是热情款待。

我在战干团学员队的一个教员是政治部第二处的顾问。实际上是他，而不是杨尔瑛，指导第二处的政治工作。他给我们的第一项任务是，调查西安城里的社团情况。我们发现，西安有大量不为人知的社会团体。早在国共两党联合北伐时，许多团体就已经存在了。1927年国共分裂，亲共组织转入地下或处于休眠状态。我们做调查时，一些组织的领导人还健在。一些人还是社区领袖，在动员民众抗战上可以发挥作用。

虽是战时，但并不表示所有地区都有战事。很长一段时间，北方战线都很平静。1939年9月，我决定重拾学业。

胡将军同意后，我便从政治部辞职，去重庆参加大学统一入学考试。胡将军给了我一些盘缠。我从西安坐火车到宝鸡，然后搭汽车，来到战时陪都重庆。

汽车要走很长的路，还要翻山越岭。到达一座山顶时，我闻到了一股难闻的气味，涕泪直流。我想起此前汽车经过一户人家门前时，有人正在炸辣椒。辣椒味如此之重，熏得人不由得流泪。我还想到他家门上挂着一大串干辣椒。对贫苦的山民来说，辣椒好像就是他们的主食。

然后我看到路边墙上有两个洞。洞和洞之间的距离，刚好是前后两个轿夫间的距离。轿子是农村地区最重要的交通工具，一顶轿子，需要两个人用肩膀抬。他们经常抬着轿子走很远的路。为保持体力，轿夫需要吸鸦片。但是，把轿子放下再进鸦片馆是件麻烦事。于是他们就把轿子沿着路边墙垣停下来，转过头，两个人的嘴各自对着墙上的两个洞，洞里伸出鸦片烟斗，他们就能吸了。轿夫们就站在那里抽完几口鸦片，补充精力后继续抬轿前行。

衣、食、住、行是人生四大必需品。战争让我有机会亲身观察到内地穷人真实的生活状况，这不禁让我思考：赢得战争和改善人民的生活水平相比，究竟哪个更重要？

选
专
业

我从宝鸡坐了两天汽车，在成都稍作停留，便来到战时陪都重庆参加大学入学考试。彼时，中国公立大学的入学考试都是统一招考的，私立大学可以自己招考。国立中央大学是当时中国最大的大学，著名的私立大学复旦大学也在重庆。我同时报考了这两所学校。在统考的制度里，申请人被分成三类：第一类是理工科的学生；第二类是农医科的学生；第三类是人文和社会科的学生。我年轻时父亲对我的教诲是要学理工富强中国，我在省内上中学时也学理科。但是我不能考第一类，因为第一类的考试科目中有微积分，而我从没学过，那是高三的课程。我念完高二后就投笔从戎，没有念高三，所以微积分要得零分。如果考第一类，一定考不上。

于是我决定报考第三类，首选国立中央大学历史系。报考前，我向中大历史系三年级的王琳同学请教。他强烈反对我报考历史系，理由是学历史是为了解、认知整个世界，而不仅仅是中国。因此，我必须先掌握一门外语。听了他的意见，我便选了国立中央大学外文系，同时还报考了复旦大学历史地理系。两所大学我都考取了。国立中央大学是免费的，复旦大学收学费。作为贫穷的难民学生，我选了国立中央大学。

实际上，早在考试通过前，我就已经住在国立中央大学的宿舍里了。我到重庆后，无地可投宿，我去拜访马秀权小姐。她是马星野教授的妹妹，而马教授是我父亲在高中教过的一位学生。秀权当时是国立中央大学大四的学生，住在学校宿舍里。我告诉她我需要找个安身之地，她说她可以帮我在男生宿舍找张床位。大四学生宿舍里当时有一些空床位，因为学生要么已经结婚，要么找到工作，就搬出去了。所以在成为国立中央大学的新生前，我就像大四学生一样生活在学校的宿舍里了。

隐居的新生

我像隐士一般，开始了新生的生活。国立中央大学把新生安置在位于一个叫柏溪的村庄的分校里。柏溪当时几乎没人住，完全与世隔绝。从河岸到校园的路上，只有一家小商店。店主和他的家人照看着店铺。除了这几个人外，偶尔有乡姑农妇上门到我的同学处收取换洗衣服。我不知道她们是不是村里人。这就是我在柏溪见到的人，剩下的就是国立中央大学的新生和教职员工了。

柏溪没有路。要进出，必须走一段乡间小道，然后翻过一座山。在主校区和柏溪分校间穿梭教学的老师，往往坐轿子而不是走路。轿子由两个轿夫抬着。我们学生享受不起这样的奢侈。

出柏溪有另一条路，就是坐船。嘉陵江发源于四川北部的山区，在重庆和长江汇合。柏溪就坐落在嘉陵江边。汽轮不时会沿江而下，搭载沿江城市的一些旅客。但柏溪没有汽轮停靠的码头。要乘汽轮得先坐一段小舢板，等小舢板靠近汽轮一侧再登船。汽轮不会放慢速度等人，上船并不容易。

　　嘉陵江河道很浅，并不是全年都可以通航，有时我们坐不上汽轮。只有到了夏天或雨季，汽轮方可通行。坐汽轮相当危险，经常发生翻船事故。

　　嘉陵江水流湍急。为避免受困于船舱而产生幽闭恐惧症，多数旅客喜欢站在汽轮的甲板上，汽轮便头重尾轻。遇到弯道急拐，经常会翻船。

　　沿江有一些舢板，有些很靠近翻沉了的汽轮。舢板很容易捞起落水的旅客，但几乎没有人被救起。四川船民非常迷信，他们认为，如果阎王选择让一个人溺水而死，救人之举是违背阎王的意愿的。他救了人，阎王会让他做替死鬼。所以没人敢救溺水的。这也是坐船的一个风险。

　　避免翻船溺死的唯一办法，就是会游泳。要坐船，我得先学会游泳。柏溪没有游泳池，也没有人教我游泳。我就到江边找一个水浅的岸滩，自己试着学游泳，终于学会了。我游得不快，但能游很长一段距离。后来我可以游400码（合366米），和嘉陵江的宽度一样。这样，坐船就有安全感了，不管船在哪里翻沉，我都能够游到岸边。

有时候我也坐大木船，木船满载着橘子沿江而下去重庆。坐这样的船是一种愉悦的体验，因为东家会让我随便吃橘子而不用掏钱，唯一的条件是我得把橘子皮留在甲板上，而不是扔进江里，因为橘子皮可用来当药材。船到重庆后，东家得雇人剥橘子，然后把橘子皮卖出去。我们免费吃橘子，也就意味着同时在给他免费剥橘子皮。这笔交易是互惠的。

在柏溪分校的生活艰苦。政府提供的米不够吃，我们每顿都得为饭而战。如果不能抢到一碗饭，就会饿肚子。幸运的是，四川省多产橘子和花生，价格不贵，而且营养丰富。它们养活了我们这些半饿着肚子的大学新生，让我们身体健康。

第一学年结束后，我离开了柏溪，回到重庆沙坪坝的主校区，开始二年级的生活。在这里，再也不用忍受各种生活的不便和痛苦了，可以吃上米饭，有地方洗澡，也能乘公共汽车到各个地方去逛。重庆和国内几个主要城市之间还有航班相通。更重要的是，我们学习到了战争的一项重要内容——空袭。

柏溪没有空袭。重庆的空袭分两种，一种是恐怖轰炸，一种是疲劳轰炸。恐怖轰炸就是许多轰炸机轰炸同一个目标，使那里的人们非常恐慌。

疲劳轰炸持续很长时间，人们躲在防空洞里，没吃没喝，也没地方躺下来休息睡觉，时间一长，就会身心俱疲。

中国那时没有防空设备，也不生产飞机。所有战斗机都是从国外买来的二手货，性能不佳，无法与日机抗衡。中国战机升空抗击日机，很可能会被击落，飞行员因此丧命。中国战机便得了个"棺材"的绰号。

　　只要政府有钱，就可以在短时间里买到更多更好的飞机。但飞行员可不是一夜之间就能培养的。中国当时训练有素的飞行员屈指可数。所以政府发布命令，不允许飞行员驾机抗击来犯日机。因此，空防就成了空白。

　　防空炮是中国当时拥有的唯一防空武器，数量不多，政府把它们主要部署在战时陪都重庆周围，此外还在重庆建立了一套防空警报系统。这套警报系统覆盖三个地理圈，第一圈是市中心外围几英里的范围。日机逼近这个空域，就会拉响第一种空袭警报，城里的居民就知道日机来了。第二圈离市中心近一些。日机抵达这个防空圈，第二种警报就会响起，人们就准备躲进防空洞。重庆是山城，岩石很硬，在街道底下凿穿岩石，就是很好的防空洞。防空洞离商店很近，便于人们躲藏。第三圈就离市中心很近了。日机进入这个防空圈时，第三种警报就拉响，人们就得跑进防空洞。很快，炸弹就在城里四面开花。

这套防空系统理论上看起来很好，但它也为日机制造了疲劳轰炸的机会。日本人知道中国战机无法攻击日军轰炸机，就一次先派一架轰炸机来袭扰，然后算好市中心和第三防空圈之间的距离，当第一架轰炸机完成它的任务，准备飞离的时候，第二架轰炸机就已经到达第三防空圈，所以重庆就不能解除警报。第二架轰炸机完成它的任务后，第三架轰炸机接着就来。日机一架接着一架不断进入防空圈，警报就无法解除，防空洞里的人也无法出来。如果空袭持续太久，里面的人就会饥渴交加，疲惫不堪，呼吸困难。

有一次，经过长时间的疲劳轰炸，因为防空洞的通风设备不好，里面的空气变得混浊，洞里的人开始感到窒息，有些人便强行跑出防空洞，却被把守在洞外的卫兵轰了回去。有些卫兵甚至拿一把大锁锁了防空洞的门。空袭结束后，卫兵打开大门，只有接近门口的少数几个人活着出来，其他人都窒息而死。

防空洞上方是街道。警报解除后，沿街商店的门都没有人开，因为店主和店员们都死在防空洞里了。全面抗战期间，这是空袭造成的最大、最惨痛的灾难。

我就读的国立中央大学，位于重庆城外，但它也是日军空袭的一个目标。有一天，27架日军战机轰炸了学校和周边地区，一颗燃烧弹落在我的宿舍，烧坏了我的蚊帐。校园里蚊虫肆虐，没有蚊帐根本无法入睡。

中国政府认识到，要防空就必须要有飞机。于是它向美国政府贷款，购买了100架战斗机，聘请了100名美国飞行员和一些空服及地勤人员。这些飞行员来自美国陆军和海军的航空兵种。他们徽章上的标志是一只带翅膀的老虎，所以被叫作"飞虎队"。下一章，我来讲讲我在飞虎队的经历，虽然我从来没有飞过飞机。

飞虎队

第一批飞虎队的官方名称是"美国志愿兵"。1941年，我加入飞虎队。

飞虎队是由中国政府从美国政府贷款创建的，它是中国空军的一部分，不属于美国空军。由于当时美国和日本不是交战国，美国不能派其空军帮中国对日作战。尽管这些飞行员来自美国陆军和海军，他们却因此被称作"美国志愿兵"。

除了100名美国战斗机飞行员和队长克莱尔·李·陈纳德上校外，飞虎队成员还包括飞行机械师、无线电报务员、情报人员、一名医生、一名护士、一位秘书，还有一位副队长。他们都是美国人，所以得配备翻译。中国空军没有那么多翻译可提供。虽然国内当时有许多会英语的人有能力为飞虎队当翻译，但出于担心日本间谍借机渗透，中国空军不敢公开招聘翻译人员。于是政府下令，要求国内五所顶尖大学英语系的学生，自愿为飞虎队当翻译，为期一年。期满可返回学校就读于原来的班级。于是，在整个抗战时期，我第二次自愿报了名（上次是自愿到第一军当兵）。

　　加入飞虎队当翻译前，我们接受了 3 个月培训，学习了一些空军专用术语，了解了中美关系，掌握了英国英语和美国英语的差别。我们也掌握了一些美国俚语。但有一个词我们一直没学过，那就是美军无线电报务员几乎句句不离口的"他妈的"（Fuck）。后来，我在飞虎队总部工作，美军无线电报务员打电话告诉我有陈纳德上校的电文时，我都很难听明白他的话，因为他话里夹杂了太多"他妈的"。

　　培训结束后，我被分到陈纳德上校办公室，任翻译兼密码译电员。8 个译电员，分成 4 个组，每组 2 人，每组每天工作 6 小时。译电室通宵达旦工作。我们对来往的所有电报进行解码或译成密码。密码很简单。两个数字代表一个字母。比如，"45216876345698245532"代表"日本人来了"（Japs coming），其中 45 代表 J，21 代表 a，68 代表 p，76 代表 s，34 代表 c，等等。密码本三个月一换。我一直认为，日本人没能破译我们的密码，看不懂它们的意思。

飞虎队总部设在昆明机场的一幢小楼里，只有四个房间。陈纳德上校的办公室里，有英文秘书、中文秘书舒伯炎上校和他自己。舒上校同时是翻译主任，也是我的顶头上司。陈纳德上校办公室隔壁是译电室——译电员工作的地方。他对面是飞虎队副队长格林上尉的办公室。格林上尉办公室隔壁是客厅，接待访客的地方。

陈纳德来上班时，就把车停在楼外。他的中国司机一整天就待在车里待命。译电员要去电台取电报，交通处会派司机开着小车或吉普来总部，送译电员去。

刚开始，飞虎队驾驶的是P-40战斗机。它的性能和速度要胜过日机。陈纳德向飞虎队队员传授了攻击日机的技巧。P-40升空后，日军战斗机很难击落它。大多数P-40战斗机都坠毁在缅北战场。那里的防空警报系统不完善，日机有时会趁P-40战斗机起飞前悄然来犯，这样，地面上的飞机就会被炸毁。

1941 年，正当我们这些翻译人员受训之际，日军轰炸了珍珠港，美国随即对日宣战。中国政府要求美国人派遣空军来华，以替换飞虎队。之后，美国第 14 陆军航空兵来到中国，中美两国飞行员组建了联合空军。陈纳德担任了联合空军的领导职务，所以他们后来也自称"飞虎队"。但他们不像我，没有"飞虎队"的徽章。

飞虎队总部后来从昆明迁到重庆。我在空军一年的自愿服务期已满。当时，我面临两个选择：要么在空军待着，要么回学校继续上学。我选择了后者。但学校不同意我回到原来的年级上课。我不得不补上过去一年没有上的所有课程，晚一年才毕业。

1944 年，我从国立中央大学毕业后，就考进重庆新闻学院。我将另起一章讲述重庆新闻学院的故事，让我先讲完和飞虎队相关的故事。

　　多年后，我在美国斯坦福大学胡佛研究所东亚图书馆当研究员兼馆长时，我当年在飞虎队的顶头上司舒伯炎上校来到加州旧金山。1958 年，陈纳德上校去世。我问舒是否认识陈纳德夫人，他回答说认识。事实上，陈夫人当年作为报社记者，曾经采访过陈纳德。采访就在陈纳德的办公室里进行，舒上校当时也在场，随时准备提供协助。

　　我请舒上校帮我一个忙，给陈夫人写封信，让她把陈纳德的个人档案交给胡佛研究所保管。他同意了。

　　陈夫人的回信直接寄给了我。她在信里说，无法提供陈纳德的档案，因为西点军校和美国国家档案馆此前提出了同样的请求。胡佛研究所和上述两所机构相比，当时只能排第三。收信后，我立即给陈夫人回复，告诉她，我有三个很好的理由要得到陈纳德的个人档案。

　　首先，我当过陈纳德的译电员，帮他解码和编码了很多来往的电报。他的档案也是我的档案。我会很好地保管它。

其次，保管档案的目的是为了让学者和研究人员能够接触到它，写本好书，或完成一项重要的研究项目。作为军事院校，学者和研究人员不容易接触到西点的图书馆，陈纳德的档案也就难以物尽其用。国家档案馆馆藏丰富，个人档案只能湮没在其中。我没明说的是，和保管在那里的许多要人的档案相比，陈纳德的档案只能算沧海一粟。第三个理由最重要。陈纳德的政治对手是维内加·乔，即约瑟夫·史迪威将军。史迪威将军的档案在胡佛研究所。美国著名记者白修德（西奥多·哈罗德·怀特）正是利用史迪威的档案编写了一本畅销书，书名就叫《史迪威文件》。陈纳德在那本书里的形象并不是很正面。修正陈纳德在历史中的形象很重要，陈纳德的夫人有义务这么做。我告诉她，如果她把陈纳德的档案交给我，我会把它放在史迪威档案旁边，让学者和研究人员了解他俩的观点。史迪威的观点会被修正，陈纳德的立场也会被人们理解和认知。

　　过了几天，我接到陈纳德夫人的电话。她告诉我，会在某一天坐某个时刻的航班，亲自把她丈夫的档案捎给我。她要我到旧金山机场接机。几天后，胡佛研究所召开了记者会，宣布接管陈纳德的档案。从那以后，每年第一个给我寄新年贺卡的就是陈纳德夫人，她的名字叫陈香梅。

　　1944年，我从国立中央大学英文系毕业后，就想找机会出国深造。当时中国高等教育不发达，中国学生到国外接受高等教育很重要。对英语专业的学生来说，到美国、英国等英语国家接受高等教育尤其重要。

　　出国留学费用很高。父亲不能再资助我，因为他生活在上海日占区，而且没有了工作。中国政府也已经多年没有向出国学英语的留学生提供奖学金了。穷学生出国留学深造的唯一途径就是想办法通过外交领事官员的资格考试，在外交部谋得一岗半职，工作几年后，也许能够被外派。如果有幸被派到一个教育发达的国家，就可以上夜课，拿到高等学位。每年，几乎所有英语专业的大学毕业生都会参加外交部入部考试。外交部每年的空缺有限，而报考的毕业生人数众多，所以考入外交部很难。

　　1944年，我大学毕业时，中日还在交战。政府不仅军事力量薄弱，在提供和传播国际新闻方面也是如此。蒋介石指示国民党中央宣传部副部长董显光加强战时新闻服务的力量。为此，中国需要相当数量有能力又懂英语的新闻官员。可惜当时人数不够，董博士于是决定招募和培训一批人。

董显光博士毕业于纽约市的哥伦比亚大学新闻学院。哥大新闻学院时任院长阿克曼博士恰好是他的同班同学。于是他去哥大看望阿克曼院长，跟他探讨培训新闻官员的事宜。他们同意为此在中国成立一所新闻学院。哥大向该学院派遣5名教授，董博士负责招生。

为了找到最好的英语专业学生，董博士在重庆、成都和昆明报纸上刊登招生启事，通告如下：

1. 学校名称定为：重庆新闻学院；

2. 学院聘有美国教授；

3. 所有大学毕业生都可报考；

4. 录取 30 名研究生；

5. 学制一年；

6. 学生毕业后须在国民党中央宣传部国际新闻处工作一年；

7. 一年期满，前 10 名毕业生可获奖学金赴美深造。

上述条件显然要比外交部提供的待遇好很多。董博士将学院入学考试安排在和外交部入部考试同一天。英语专业最好的学生几乎都报考了重庆新闻学院。

很幸运，我通过了入学考试，被录取了。学院的课程基本上和哥伦比亚大学新闻学院的课程相同。为了训练英文报道，我们出版了一份名为《重庆新闻》的英文周报。这份报纸被分送给在中国的所有外国记者，还被寄给美国国会图书馆、国会议员和美国政府的许多高级官员。虽然没有获得普利策新闻奖，它却起到了传播战时中国国际新闻的作用。

（续）
重庆新闻学院

在建院前，重庆新闻学院附属于国立政治大学。当时也只能这样，因为根据那时中国的教育法，研究生院必须隶属于一所大学，不能独立设置。于是我们也就成了国立政治大学的学生。新闻学院在重庆城里，在地域上和位于南温泉村的国立政治大学相距甚远。两校的行政管理和财政各自独立。国立政治大学美国校友会把我们视作其会员，但我们很少参加他们的活动。

重庆新闻学院建院后，哥伦比亚大学新闻学院派出了包括院长在内的五名教授。董显光博士任中方院长，曾虚白任副院长，还有三位中方教员：国立政治大学新闻系主任马星野教授中国新闻史；外交部副部长甘乃光教授国际关系学；国民党中央执行常委潘公展教授党的原则，这也是所有大学生的必修课。第二年，哥大新闻学院美方院长回美国去了，美国报纸资深驻华记者甘露德（罗德尼·扬克斯·吉尔伯特）出任新的美方院长。哥大向重庆新闻学院增派了一位助理教授。

这样一来，我们30个学生就有了6位教授，每位教授管理5个学生。每天早上9时上课，每个同学分到一项任务。任务包括：采访有新闻价值的人；参加公共活动；调查社会或政治事件；听一些要人或名人演讲。接到任务后，我们就离校干活。活干完了，赶紧回校准备报告。我们必须在下午5时前向主管教授提交报告，晚一分钟也不行。期限就是期限，如果不能按时完成，报告就会得零分。教授收到报告后，会让每个学生坐在他旁边看他修改。教授会按作出的修改给报告打分。

　　写得好的报道会被学生们为加强训练而出版的《重庆新闻》英文周报采用。我们并没有写出很多有意思的报告。但有一份报告真的对政府产生了影响。中国从来没有新闻法，政府想立个法。新闻法公布前，我的一个同学找到了这份法律的稿本，把它登在了《重庆新闻》上。外国驻华记者看到了，感到很震惊，因为它严重限制了新闻自由。在战时，有些条款可能是必要的，但和平时期就不会被接受。于是外国记者向政府表示抗议。结果，这份新闻法案便胎死腹中。

战时并不意味着每时每刻都会有战争。二战期间，中国战区很长一段时间都没有发生激烈的战斗。在中国的战地记者的生活就变得枯燥无趣。为了让他们摆脱乏味，中央宣传部国际新闻处的专员吉米·魏，一个很聪明的人，突然作了个宣布。他告诉外国战地记者，在中国农历的五月初五，鸡蛋可以不必敲碎就能直立起来。他说，到了那天，他会演示给他们看。所有的战地记者都来看他表演。魏迅速地把几个而不是一个鸡蛋竖立在水泥地上。战地记者很吃惊，纷纷报道此事。这成了二战期间最广为流传的新闻之一。

实际上这不是骗人的把戏。只要不在像玻璃那样光滑的平面上，鸡蛋是可以竖立起来的。不信，你可以试试。

战争结束

从重庆新闻学院毕业后，我有两个星期的假。我哥马大恢当时在西安当胡宗南将军的便衣队队长。一俟毕业我就马上去西安看他，住在他的营房里。一天晚上，我被街上的一阵鞭炮和喧闹声惊醒。大家都在庆祝日本投降和抗战胜利。

无论从哪种角度看，抗战都是近现代中国历史上最重要的事件。2000万中国人从日本占领的沿海地区向欠发达的内地迁移。抗战期间，中国万众一心。许多内地人平生第一次认识到，中国和日本一样都是国家，他们有责任保家卫国。战争给他们上了一堂教育课。

我提前结束休假，匆匆赶回重庆新闻学院，等待分配工作。美国海军陆战队此时已在北方登陆，帮助中国接受日军投降并解除其武装。一些美国记者随美军而来，中方需要公共关系官员，以便对这些战地记者有个照应。

中国政府那时在很多政府机构里设有外事办公室，但对公共关系官员办公室并没有什么概念。中国也有联络官，但从来没有公共关系官员。美国大使给蒋介石打电话，询问中方有没有公共关系官员。为不让大使失望，蒋介石马上回复说有，虽然他自己可能都没搞清楚公共关系官员是干什么的。通话完毕，蒋介石立即召来国民党中央宣传部部长，问他手底下有没有公共关系官员。部长迅即回答说有，然后打电话给董显光副部长，跟他要公共关系官员。董副部长随即致电国际新闻处处长曾虚白（曾此时兼任重庆新闻学院副院长），让他从新闻学院遴选一批毕业生，充当公共关系官员。

于是曾先生就把我们五个人叫到他办公室，告知我们已被选为公共关系官员，必须马上到北方去。我们当中的一个要去青岛，美国第七舰队总部在那里；两个要去天津，美国海军陆战队刚在那里登陆；还有一个被打发去东北，但无法成行，因为俄国军队当时还驻扎在那里；我去北京，当时叫北平。北平是蒋介石北方行营总部所在地，也是美国在华海军陆战队琼斯将军的总部。

我在北京饭店落了脚。北京饭店前身是一家法国饭店，有一个法国名字。饭店的餐厅只供应法国餐。我住在 319 房间，是饭店里最大的房间。日军占领北平期间，这个房间属于日方经理专用。我还掌握了饭店另外 2 个房间，只要战地记者有需要，我随时可以提供。我在附近的饭店还有 3 个房间备用。

　　美军战地记者想采访中方任何人，我都可以安排会见。当时北平最高当局是李宗仁将军，他是蒋介石北平行营主任。我带了一个美军战地记者去见他。李宗仁此前是广西的一个军阀，有不少军队听他的指挥，但他的军队不在北平。北平当时驻扎着胡宗南的第 34 集团军。李宗仁后来一度出任（国民政府）"代总统"。但蒋介石从未放弃过对政府包括军队和财政的控制。共产党夺取大陆政权后，李宗仁出走美国，后来又返回大陆定居。

　　美军在北平的多数战地记者经验丰富，他们并不怎么需要从我这里得到帮助。多数时间，我都待在饭店房间里看看书。有一天，我下楼想去看看饭店里的商店有什么东西可买。在问询台后面，我看到一个房间门上挂着"公共关系官员"（PRO）的指示牌，我很困惑。因为我知道，除了我，这个饭店再无其他公共关系官员。于是我就问问询台的职员那是什么房间。职员叫我别出声，悄悄说："那可是美国大兵找妓女的地方！"

阎王要开会，要我去出席，

但是我不去，阎王请勿逼。

我贪吃懒做，已被判无期。

刑期满了后，我就来看你。

2016年5月7日　作者写于美国加州阿拉梅达

175

马歇尔的使命

抗战结束也就是内战开始。国民党在全国范围发起了全面内战。蒋介石命令日本军队只向国民党军队投降。不管怎样，共产党军队也接受了日军投降。

共产党军队封锁了铁路，国民党军队无法到达中国北方的许多城市。于是美国飞机就被用来运送国民党军队去北方的一些主要城市，但飞机运送数量很有限。只有胡宗南将军的精锐部队第34集团军被空运至北平。

一天，胡将军的参谋刘向杰上校来到北平。我问他此行有何使命。他说最重要的任务是改编伪南京政府的傀儡军队。伪南京政府在战时和日本人沆瀣一气。日本人投降后，伪南京政府垮台，其为数众多的军队顿时变得群龙无首，军饷也断了。国共两党都需要这些人。国民党想通过提供军饷、给其指挥官加官晋爵来争取他们。刘上校北平之行的任务就是给亲国民党的傀儡指挥官颁发更高军阶的委任状。虽然他自己只是一名上校，但有政府授权，他可以授予一名伪军官少将军阶，少将一般是师长的军阶。

国民党用这些傀儡军队在全国各地打内战。美国总统杜鲁门决定派遣马歇尔将军来华调停国共内战，所谓"马歇尔计划"。

调停开始，建立了一个三人委员会——由美国的马歇尔、国民党的张群将军（后来被张治中将军取代）和共产党的周恩来组成。委员会达成了停战协议，在北京协和医院设立了停战执行委员会（也称军事调处执行部，简称军调部）。军调部在全国几个地方设有分部。某时某地发生了武装冲突，军调部就会派出工作组，监督实施停火。军调部每周派一次飞机向地方分部运送补给，外国记者也可随机前往战场实地调查，收集信息。

一次，法国《费加罗报》的一名记者想到张家口采访聂荣臻将军，我陪他同往。聂荣臻曾在法国学习过。采访全程，他们两人都用法语交流，这让没学过法语的我目瞪口呆。

聂将军把我们安顿在城外一个日本人修建的酒店里。第二天起床时，我问法国记者前一晚休息得怎么样。他说压根儿就没睡觉，整晚都有东西在咬他。那是臭虫，是他在巴黎或北平都没领教过的。

张家口是共产党当时在中国关内最大的城市。我在城里看到一些士兵，他们扛着各式步枪——有德国人在山东造的，有日本人造的三八大盖，也有中国各省生产制造的。其中有些枪械粗制滥造，十发子弹打完后，枪管就会很烫，手都握不住。但士兵们看上去很有精神，比国民党兵有精神。

在张家口我碰到了著名的女作家丁玲和周而复。他们可能在为《晋察冀日报》工作。他们给了我最新的几期报纸。我读到一则报道：共产党士兵站在山东省的海岸边，等待着史迪威将军领导的美国第九军登陆。他们知道史迪威将军会给他们提供美式装备。但最终他们还是白等了，因为日本人在史迪威将军登陆前就投降了。

从张家口回北平的途中，飞机计划在归绥（现呼和浩特）停留。飞行员正准备降落时，突然发现跑道太短。他迅速抬拉飞机。好在跑道尽头只是平坦的沙漠而没有建筑物，飞机得以从沙漠上空滑过，顺利升空，从而避免了机毁人亡。我逃过一劫。

　　内战蔓延到东北。军调部在吉林长春设立分部。我应邀出任军调部长春分部新闻处主任。长春（"新京"）是伪满洲国的首都，1931年日军占领东北后，在长春扶持了伪满政权，溥仪是伪满洲国皇帝。日本人本想给他造个宫殿，但直到投降，也只打好了地基。后来，中国著名的建筑大师梁思成在那个地基上盖了座房子。这座房子后来为长春地质学院所用。

　　那时，林彪是东北共产党军队的最高指挥官。一些外国记者想采访他。于是我安排了一架飞机，带他们去哈尔滨。飞机要起飞前，《大公报》的一个记者来找我，请求我也带他一起去。飞机上已没有空位，我就把我的座位让给他。他很感激我，但我却错过了面见林彪的机会。

当时李敏然是东北共产党的最高政治领袖。很多人不了解他的背景。其实，他就是李立三，曾一度担任中国共产党的负责人。他在党内失势后，去了苏联。他很可能是随苏联红军一起回到东北的。

国共双方都认为自己能打赢战争，因此，落实停战就变得很困难。国民党军队，主要是史迪威将军训练的新一军和新六军，曾经成功占领长春，还一度在松花江北岸建立了滩头阵地。但他们无法向北挺进哈尔滨，因为在人数上不敌共产党军队。

一天，吉林省省长梁华盛将军设宴招待我们。十个人的圆桌，坐了好几个戴着军长徽章的人。我知道长春附近只有新一军和新六军，它们的军长分别是郑洞国和廖耀湘。我就问他们，怎么突然冒出来这么多军长呢？他们都笑了，并告诉我，为了欺骗共产党军队，他们把两个军所有师长的军阶都提升了。每个军下辖三个师，所以一共有八个军长，而不是两个。他们以为，这样共产党军队就可能会相信国民党军队人数要比实际的多。"兵不厌诈"是中国著名的谚语，这些军人在战场上用上了。

我在长春时，杜鲁门总统派了他的私人代表埃德温·温德尔·波利到东北，调查苏军占领东北对工业经济造成的损害，包括拆卸、毁坏和掠夺工业设备的情况。我陪着美方代表团视察了几个工厂，以及向东北几乎所有大城市供电的小丰满大型水电站。波利后来在给杜鲁门总统的报告中说，预计苏军造成的损失达 20 亿美金。

结束在军调部长春分部的工作后，我返回北平，继续担任公共关系官员的职务。不久，国共两党的停战协议被撕毁，马歇尔的使命失败。他返回了美国，我则去了南京。国民党中央宣传部国际新闻处也改名为"行政院新闻局"，总部从重庆迁回了南京。按照重庆新闻学院当初的招聘公告，我们毕业后只需在中央宣传部国际新闻处服务一年，服务期满，前十名的毕业生会得到赴美留学的奖学金。我在国际新闻处已经工作一年多了，而且名列十名之内。于是，1947 年，我回到南京，等着拿奖学金。

　　1947 年，我在南京等待赴美留学奖学金时，宋子文任国民政府"行政院长"。政府当时外汇严重短缺。宋子文下了一道命令，指示未经他的允许，任何人不得持有超过 2000 美金的外汇。我的奖学金是 3500 美金，我们 10 个人的奖学金总额就是 35000 美金。如果宋子文不同意，我们赴美留学的美梦就会泡汤。我们一直等着他的批准，但是我们的申请却石沉大海。

　　有一天，我们向在新闻局工作的美国顾问提起这事，告诉他重庆新闻学院的招生广告和政府在我们一年服务期满后会提供奖学金的承诺，以及宋子文一声令下就取消了我们奖学金的来龙去脉。美国顾问对中国政府不信守承诺感到很吃惊。他对我们说，蒋夫人宋美龄当晚要宴请外国顾问，他会见到她，要把这事告诉蒋夫人——宋子文的妹妹。

第二天上午，我们接到上海中国银行来的电话，说银行有 10 张面值分别为 3500 美金的支票等着我们去取。这足以说明蒋夫人的工作效率有多高！

蒋夫人不仅帮我们搞定了奖学金的钱，还要教我们美国人的生活方式。她要求她能干的助理黄仁霖将军为我们安排一次宴会，以便教授我们餐桌礼仪。黄仁霖把我们带到一家西餐厅，叫了炸鸡块。我们只能用刀叉吃饭。在切鸡块时，其中有个同学手滑了一下，一块鸡肉就飞过桌子，砸到了对面的人。炸鸡一下子成了"飞鸡"。

我们拿到了支票。这些支票可以在中国直接兑换成现金。那时中国通货膨胀严重，3500 美金可以买很多东西。我们中的一个人，就决定不去美国了，把钱投到生意上去。他小赚了一笔。

我们这些想去美国的人，就面临着从美国总领事馆拿到签证的问题。为防止肺结核病患者进入美国，领事馆要求每个申请人提供 X 光片。我在重庆新闻学院时得过肋膜炎，X 光片可能会照出我的肺瘢痕。因此我很犹豫要不要照 X 光片。我的一个好朋友熊向晖，那时和我一样申请赴美签证。他的个头和我差不多。他自告奋勇以我的名字去照了 X 光片，把片子交给我。于是，我拿着他的 X 光片，顺利获得了签证。

　　他和我哥都是胡宗南将军在战时的随从副官。胡将军给了他们俩各 1800 美金，资助他们赴美留学。1947 年夏天，我们三人同行，一起搭船赴美。马大恢和我去了威斯康星大学，熊向晖去了克里夫兰的西储大学。由此，我告别中国，开始了在美国背井离乡的生活。

晓镜但愁云鬓改

夜吟应觉月光寒

蓬山此去无多路

青鸟殷勤为探看

作者手书

相見時難別亦難

东风无力百花残

春蚕到死丝方尽

蜡炬成灰泪始干

我和马大恢复从旧金山坐火车去了麦迪逊，到威斯康星大学报到。熊向晖则去了俄亥俄州克里夫兰的西储大学。

我在威斯康星大学新闻学院读研究生，续修在重庆新闻学院所学的专业。教授们对我都很好，我可能是威大新闻学院第一个来自中国的研究生。1948年夏，我顺利毕业，获得新闻学硕士学位。

哈佛大学和纽约哥伦比亚大学都给了我免收学费的奖学金。我因为有一个表叔在纽约，就决定到哥伦比亚大学去。

哥伦比亚大学有新闻学院，但没有新闻学博士的学位项目。因为过去做过公共关系方面的工作，我就改学国际关系。

后记

正如序言所说，这本小书是应『子女之命』而写，本意是想告诉在美国出生、长大并接受教育的儿女们，他（她）们的父亲和祖辈来自哪里，根在哪里，有哪些主要经历和人生感悟；当年的中国和现在的中国又有着怎样的环境差异，以起到某种传承之用。这些篇章是我从纽约法拉盛搬到加州旧金山以后，用电脑陆续逐字敲打出来的。文字简单，篇幅简短，但所记所叙皆出于自身经历和见闻。当然，文责自负。

鉴于年事已高，记忆力消退，来美后的经历难以在此一一陈述。所以这不能算是完整意义上的自传。且允许我在此补记到美国后的简要历程，以便让读者有全面把握。

1947年夏天，我和马大恢、熊向晖搭上美国运兵船『梅乐斯将军』号抵达旧金山。

我在胡佛研究院待了近十年。荷兰莱顿大学汉学院院长到斯坦福大学来参观，同时邀请我到他的汉学院当图书馆馆长。我在荷兰也待了将近十年。其间，参观了欧洲许多国家的汉学图书馆，创立了欧洲汉学图书馆协会，调查了欧洲的汉学图书馆，出版了一个报告。

莱顿大学和北京大学有交换学者项目。我以交换学者的资格回过中国好几次。每次都参观好些大学图书馆，觉得中国大学图书馆里的英文藏书实在太少了，退休以后就决定创立『赠书中国计划』，收集北美退休教授和学者的藏书，送给中国的大学图书馆。十年来已经送了40个集装箱的书籍给中国的大学。

知识就是力量。一国的知识量某种意义上也是国力强弱的体现。我希望『赠书中国我的运气很不好。1948年开始学国际关系，第二年中美关系就断绝了。我又改行学图书馆学。

那时候我已经没有钱念书了，就开始在纽约的布道研究图书馆工作。晚上和暑期选课，用两年时间念一年的课程，毕业后就升任布道研究图书馆副馆长。

1961年，康奈尔大学图书馆要发展中文图书，就请我去。我在那里待了四年，将中文馆藏从2,000种增加到400,000册。

1965年，斯坦福大学胡佛研究院东亚图书馆馆长吴文津被哈佛大学请去当哈佛燕京图书馆馆长。胡佛研究院就请我去接替他的位置。

191

这份『家书』才得以面世，接受读者审视。

赵世人承担了将本书从英文翻译成中文的工作，还受我委托负责和出版社沟通选题、编辑和出版等事宜。

马大任　写于加州旧金山　2016年11月5日

计划』能帮助中国的高校和科研机构增加一些知识。

我这个老愚公已经过了96岁，体力大不如前，以后能为祖国做的事恐怕很有限。

只希望我三个很能干的孩子看了这本小书后，记得他们是华裔，要为中华民族做些事，使中华民族在世界上的地位不断提高。

这本小书付梓，要感谢外语教学与研究出版社的蔡剑峰社长和吴浩先生，他们的理解与支持使之从当初的一种设想成为现实。感谢本书的责任编辑和许多未曾谋面的编辑们，她们认真的精神和负责的态度，让我这个老图书馆员都为之感动。感谢我在中国外交部工作的朋友和老乡赵世人先生，正是他当初的提议，